LOWER THAN THE ANGELS

Questions raised by Genesis 1–11

The Bible Reading Fellowship

BRF encourages regular, informed Bible-reading as a means of renewal in the churches.

BRF publishes introductory booklets on Bible-reading, group study guides, training aids, audio-visual material, etc.

BRF issues various series of regular Bible readings with explanatory notes.

Write or call now for full list of publications and services.

The Bible Reading Fellowship

St. Michael's House	P.O. Box M	Belconnen Churches Centre
2 Elizabeth Street	Winter Park	Benjamin Way
London SW1W 9RQ	Florida 32790	Belconnen ACT 2617
	U.S.A.	Australia

LOWER THAN THE ANGELS

Questions raised by Genesis 1–11

Anthony Phillips

Chaplain and Fellow, St John's College, Oxford

The Bible Reading Fellowship

In gratitude to the people
of the Good Shepherd Church,
Arbury, Cambridge among whom
I first preached the word
and celebrated the sacraments.

First published 1983

© BRF 1983

British Library CIP data

Phillips, Anthony
   Lower than the angels.
   1. Bible.O.T.Genesis I–XI—Commentaries
   I. Title
   222'.1107   BS1235.3

ISBN 0–900164–60–3

Printed by Bocardo & Church Army Press Ltd, Cowley, Oxford

Cover picture: St John's College, Oxford MS 61 Bestiary (reproduced by kind permission of the President and Fellows).

Foreword

By the Archbishop of York
Dr Stuart Blanch

This is an important book by a distinguished Old Testament Scholar. It is important because it makes available to the general reader the fruits of many generations of specialist studies. It is important because it could help to liberate the puzzled believer from the straitjacket of dogmatic and often ill-founded opinion. But above all it is important because it succeeds in presenting the early chapters of Genesis within the developing process of Israel's history and theology. It can never be said too often that the book of Genesis in its final form is the work of a profound theologian grappling with some of the most troublesome, yet creative, problems of the human race. This is more than a book about Genesis 1 to 11; it is a book about humanity and about us. I hope you will enjoy it and I am sure that you will profit from it.

Stuart Ebor:

Bishopthorpe, York
31st January 1983

CONTENTS

Foreword

Preface

Chronological Table

PREFACE

Some time ago, I interviewed for the BBC the actor then playing Jesus Christ Superstar. We talked about his understanding of the role, and whether his playing of Jesus had in any way affected him. He had clearly been moved by the figure of Jesus, but he told me that he could not become a Christian for it would mean believing in Adam and Eve and all that. In spite of a century of biblical criticism since Darwin, the actor's views remain widespread—sometimes encouraged by those Christians who hold that if some incidents in the Bible are held to be untrue, in the sense that they did not happen as it is said that they happened, then what guarantee is there that any incident actually occurred as recorded? This is a question which must be faced both as to the Old and New Testaments. For no part of scripture is to be protected from honest enquiry. But my concern is only with the first eleven chapters of Genesis which, although set out as the beginnings (= 'Genesis') of the story of the history of man's salvation, are also a timeless presentation of man's situation in the world which God has created. Adam is not some distant relative whom one can acknowledge or not as one likes: *adam* is everyman. Genesis 1–11 is not just a primitive people's account of their origins: it is an analysis of what it means to be human, an uncomfortable analysis which we ignore at our peril. But Genesis 1–11 is also a proclamation of gospel, good news, for it is an analysis too of the God with whom *adam* has to deal, who destined man for fellowship with him in an ordered world, and who will not let him go. Whether man chooses to accept this is of course a matter of faith. But it is my experience that all too often men are not in a position to make such a decision, for they are asking the wrong question: Is Genesis 1–11 fact or fiction? It is the purpose of this book by asking a number of questions so to unravel the theology of Genesis 1–11 as to enable everyman to be confronted by the fundamental question which these chapters pose: Have you the courage to believe in your own salvation?

The title of the book comes from the Authorised Version's rendering of Psalm 8:4–5:

> What is man, that thou art mindful of him? and the son of man, that thou visitest him?
> For thou hast made him a little lower than the angels, and hast crowned him with glory and honour.

This is a translation of the ancient Greek version of the Hebrew scriptures known as the Septuagint completed during the first century BC. But in the original Hebrew text—from which the Greek translators shied away—man is boldly described as made 'lower than the *elohim*', the general Hebrew word for God or gods. In other words, the Psalmist saw man alone of all created life as intimately related to God himself. As he indicates in the rest of the Psalm, in spite of man's apparent insignificance when considering the wonders of God's creation, he is none the less directly appointed as God's vice-regent, and given dominion over the natural world. So far then as the created order is concerned, there is no limit into what *adam* may enquire, for the heavens and earth are his to control. This was the divine command given to man, made in the image of God, at creation (Gen. 1).

But Genesis 1–11 goes on to indicate that while, as the Psalmist saw, man was God's appointed vice-regent, he remains man. He was not present at creation, but is a result of it. He cannot then penetrate what lies behind creation—the divine realm, heaven itself (Gen. 11). In the relationship between God and man, God remains God and man man. But while man cannot know as God knows (otherwise he would be God), and must be content to be agnostic about some things (e.g. the origin of evil) and suffer death (Gen. 2–3), unlike the animals he can know God. This is the tension of being *adam*. And in so far as we fail to appropriate this gift of relationship with God, then we are less than human. This is why Christians regard Jesus as the perfect *adam*, for he alone of all men fully grasped his full human potential in his perfect relationship with his Father in which he did not grasp at divinity (Philippians 2:6), but was content to die as man, an agnostic believer:

My God, my God, why hast thou forsaken me?

It is into this tension of knowing and not knowing, of being like God but not God—a little lower than the immortal angels who were understood to know what was going on in the divine realm—that all men are born. This is what it is to be *adam*.

I have assumed that the reader is familiar with the text of Genesis 1–11. It would, however, be advisable to read it in more than one English version. Biblical references are to the English text, and not the Hebrew.

Oxford   Anthony Phillips
September 1981

CHRONOLOGICAL TABLE

Date	Event	Kings	Prophets	Literary Works
1000		David (1000–961)		
	On Solomon's death separate kingdoms of Israel in the north under Jeroboam I (capital Samaria) and Judah in the south under Rehoboam (capital Jerusalem) were formed.	Solomon (c. 961–922)		J, the first strand of the Pentateuch, written.
750			Amos Hosea	
721	Fall of Samaria to the Assyrians and the end of the northern kingdom of Israel. Hezekiah of Judah institutes his reform.	Hezekiah (715–687)	Isaiah Micah	J revised in the light of the fall of the northern kingdom.
		Josiah (640–609)	Jeremiah	
621	Discovery of the law book in the temple led to the Deuteronomic reform under which all worship was centralized by Josiah at Jerusalem.			The original book of Deuteronomy composed (Deut. 4:44–30:20).
597	Fall of Jerusalem to the Babylonians and exile in Babylon of Jehoiachin and leading citizens.		Ezekiel	
586	Rebellion of Zedekiah and fall of Jerusalem to the Babylonians who destroy the temple.			
561	Release of Jehoiachin from prison.			Between 560–540 the Deuteronomic Work (Deuteronomy –2 Kings) reached its final form.

Date	Event	Kings	Prophets	Literary Works
538	Edict of Persian king, Cyrus, allowing Jews to return to Palestine from exile in Babylon.		Second Isaiah (Is. 40 –55)	Around this time, the Priestly Work (Genesis–Numbers) produced using the revised version of J.
			Trito– Isaiah (Is. 56– 66)	
500			Zechariah	Later, sometime in the late sixth or the fifth century Deuteronomy was detached from the Deuteronomic Work and attached to the Priestly Work to form the Pentateuch (Genesis– Deuteronomy).

Chapter 1

The Background to Genesis 1–11

(i)

What is Genesis 1–11 about?

Genesis 1–11 is the beginning of the story of God's redemption of man through his chosen people Israel, which Christians see completed in the incarnation, death and resurrection of Jesus Christ. With strict economy it describes the creation of an idyllic world in which all things were good (Gen. 1), and where man could enjoy perfect order in fellowship with his God (Gen. 2). But man is not content with his lot. Seeking to be like God, he disobeys the divine command and chaos results (Gen. 3). This not only leads to expulsion from the garden, but to a total breakdown of human relationships as brother murders brother. But lest God's work in creation be brought to nothing, the murderer is given divine protection (Gen. 4). Yet disorder so increases that it even goes beyond the confines of the earth to involve the divine world (Gen. 6:1–4). So God determines to start afresh: one family is chosen to survive the flood (Gen. 6–9). Yet even this divine purge cannot bring man to heel. His arrogant ambition continues to know no bounds as with his tower he seeks to penetrate the divine realm itself (Gen. 11:1–9). Again man's arrogance is followed by chaos and God is forced to turn from direct punishment to direct salvation. He calls Abraham (Gen. 12:1–3).

Genesis 1–11 is thus the introduction to all holy scripture, Jewish and Christian. But it does not merely set the scene for what is to follow: like the prologue to a Greek or Elizabethan play, it gives the plot away. For the reader is there told that despite the horrors that lie ahead, this story can yet have a happy ending: indeed that is what God wills. Within these brief chapters the entire gospel of the Hebrew scriptures is proclaimed which the gospel of the prophet from Nazareth confirms. It is as if a detective thriller contained in its opening chapter not only the discovery of the corpse, but also the identity of the killer. It means of course that the reader can understand the true significance of the rest of the story only in the light of this introduction. The whole biblical drama then takes on an inevitability which reduces what appears at first sight to be a series of unrelated events into a carefully ordained pattern in which even the genealogies

1

(Gen. 4, 5, 10, 11) play an integral part. God's will in creation can only be thwarted by lack of faith. Despite so much failure, man's proper destiny is the resumption of his proper place in the garden, to enjoy God's presence there. The ultimate victory need not lie with chaos, no matter how dreadful appearances to the contrary may seem at any one time.

(ii)

How did Genesis 1–11 reach its present form?

The story of how Genesis 1–11 reached its present form is a complex one, for it is part of the history of the making of the Pentateuch, the first five books of the Old Testament, Genesis, Exodus, Leviticus, Numbers and Deuteronomy, together known to Jews as the Torah. Traditionally *torah* is rendered in English as 'law' but it means far more than strictly legal rules and regulations, though many of these are found within the Pentateuch. Originally *torah* meant instruction or teaching on a specific point (cp. Haggai 2:10ff.), a definitive ruling, but later it came to be understood more generally in a collective sense as the complete expression of God's will for his people, all they needed to know in order to do what he wanted. Thus to call the first five books of the Bible the Torah indicates (i) that it is God's will that the Jews are his elect people; and (ii) that they contain those specific rulings whereby this people can know and obey his will in any situation which may confront them. For the Jews then the Torah was and is their most treasured possession and the source of continual joy and thanksgiving. It both assures them of God's love and gives them the means whereby they can continue in that love.

Though for centuries it was attributed to Moses, this last century of critical scholarship has shown that the Torah (or Pentateuch) is the product of a long process of writing, and before that of oral transmission, in which particular stories, traditions, laws and customs were passed down in the clans that eventually made up Israel, until they came to be ordered in writing for theological purposes. In Genesis 1–11 we have material from two major literary stages in the development of the final work, the first probably occurring some four hundred years before the second. This is not difficult to see even in an English translation of the Hebrew text. For example, Genesis 1:1–2:4a adopts an entirely different style to that of the Eden creation account (Gen. 2:4b–3:24). The former is formal, almost liturgical: the language

2

is dignified and the narrative carefully ordered, God remaining distant and transcendent. In contrast the much older Eden narrative depicts God in intimate human terms.

While some scholars argue that these two stages both produced their own independent literary works which were later combined by a redactor, it seems to me preferable to see the earlier work taken over, adapted and enlarged by the later material to form a new literary creation. It is as if a play of Shakespeare had been taken over and reworked for the twentieth-century by John Osborne. First there is some pure Osborne to make sure that the reader starts off on the right foot. Then the Shakespeare plot is used to provide the framework for the modern Osborne interpretation. This explains why there are apparently two creation accounts and two stories of the flood, though in both instances the accounts are intended to be read as one. The creation account in Genesis 1 represents the theological world of an Israel defeated and exiled in Babylon after 586 BC, an Israel which had lost temple, king and country, and which in Ezekiel's prophecy (Ezek. 37) had to be recreated from dead bones. In contrast, the story of Eden (Gen. 2:4b–3:24) comes from a literary work composed in the light of Israel's imperial splendour following the establishment of the new Davidic state by David and Solomon in the tenth century BC, when that state had taken her place among the empires of the ancient Near East and confidence knew no bounds. This story then reflects a milieu not unlike that of Queen Elizabeth I, while the background of the later creation account in Genesis 1 is nearer to the crisis of identity suffered by the Britain of Queen Elizabeth II following the loss of its empire. And the time-span between the two literary works is about the same as between the two Elizabeths. We must then expect that the world view of one work will be very different from that of the other: but the mention of Shakespeare should at least warn us to beware of imagining that the earlier work could not have had its insights which the later work confirms and complements.

(iii)

The first literary stage

The earliest literary strand of the Pentateuch is known as J from the fact that from the beginning it uses the specific Hebrew name for Israel's

God, Yahweh (Gen. 4:26), which in Germany, where this modern critical view evolved, is transliterated with a J*. Later literary strands of the Petateuch introduce this proper name for the Hebrew God only after its specific disclosure to Moses to enable him to lead the Hebrews out of Egypt (Ex. 3:13–15, 6:2–3). For J there is no break between the creation narrative and the patriarchal stories leading to the exodus from Egypt under Moses: in contrast the other strands emphasize that with Moses something new occurs.

This J account is held to have been written either in the tenth century BC during the period of the united monarchy of David and Solomon, or soon afterwards, for its purpose is to portray the monarchy as the fulfilment (2 Sam. 7:9) of the promise to Abraham (Gen. 12:1–3). It is difficult to be more precise for while the work clearly supports the Davidic monarchy it could either reflect a desire to legitimize a new system of government much questioned at its inception (1 Samuel 8, 10:17–27, 12), or it may have been prompted by the break-up of the empire after Solomon's death and the necessity to affirm the position of Davidic southern Judah in the face of the break-away northern kingdom of Israel under Jeroboam I. But in either case the style of the work reflects the brilliant court life of Solomon's Jerusalem dominated by the wise who administered his complex bureaucracy.

Alongside the priests and prophets, the wise formed a distinct class in ancient Israel (Jeremiah 18:18). Their task was to discern the order in things, how one thing related to another, how the world functioned. They were early scientists, examining both nature and man. Their conclusions were arrived at only after careful observation on the presupposition that there was a divine order to all things. It was man's task to discover this order and obey it. Then he would enjoy that full prosperity which God had ordained for him at creation. The wise at that time were incurably optimistic. It was only much later in the post-exilic biblical wisdom books of Proverbs, Job and Ecclesiastes that a different mood was to prevail as the wise questioned the existence of a moral order in the world. In the time of Solomon such an

---

* The common English form Jehovah derives from a combination of the consonants YHWH with the vowels of the noun *adonai* meaning Lord. In late Old Testament times, the Jews regarded the divine name Yahweh as so sacred that it could not be pronounced and instead read out the word for Lord. To remind them to do this they vocalized the divine name YHWH with the vowels of *adonai*. The English translators transliterated this word as Jehovah—a non-existent name.

order was assumed. His was an age of unbounded self-confidence both politically and scientifically. In our later discussion of J material in Genesis 1–11, we shall expect to find this confidence as well as the influence of the wise in strictly scientific matters.

It is not always easy to assign material to a particular source, especially when it may have been partially used again by a later author. But the following passages are generally assigned to J: Genesis 2:4b–4:26, 6:1–8, 9:18–27, 10:8–19,28–30, 11:1–9,28–30. Thus the J narrative contains the well-known stories of Adam and Eve and their expulsion from Eden, the murder of Abel by his brother Cain, the birth of the giants, and the tower of Babel. In addition parts of a J narrative of the flood can be isolated in Genesis 7:6–8:22. Whatever else may be said of J, he could certainly tell a good story. But his purpose is not simply to entertain, nor to re-tell ancient traditions and beliefs. Rather he is producing a theological explanation of the world as it appeared to him, and in particular the place of the Davidic state in God's scheme of things. The history of that state does not begin with the call of Abraham in Genesis 12:1–3, but with the creation of man himself. In other words, what J does is to bring into history the ancient stories and traditions which he inherits from whatever source, Israelite or not, and produce a work in which God is seen as acting in history from the beginning of time and towards some definite purpose. The primaeval stories thus become part of history, because it is J's belief that it is only within history that God acts. The result is that he can produce a coherent narrative in which there are no loose ends. The reader is offered an entire explanation of the nature of God, the nature of man, and the existence of the chosen people. Through the use of a minimum of ancient traditions, J shows how God intends all men to be in relation to him, but how, through man's disobedience, it is God who has to take the initiative in restoring that relationship. So the climax of J's primaeval narrative comes with the call of Abraham (Gen. 12:1–3), the father of Israel, in whom all the nations of the world will bless themselves. Israel's election is then of world significance, as the powerful Solomonic state confirms.

The effect of J is then to show that as far as God is concerned nothing can thwart his plan of salvation. The establishment of the Davidic monarchy has been realized in spite of every obstacle put in God's way. His grace cannot be exhausted: he has willed the salvation of mankind and not even man's disobedience will ultimately deter him. So in his history of salvation, J encourages the reader to rejoice.

Yahweh, God of Israel, and no other god is in control of both nature and history, for in neither does anything happen which is not part of his scheme of things.

(iv)

An alternative theology

The subsequent history of the development of the Pentateuch is notoriously complicated and controversial. For our purposes, we need not go into it in any great detail, for in Genesis 1–11 we are dealing only with the earliest and latest literary strands, and these substantially agree in their theology. Yet this final literary strand of the Pentateuch, in reaffirming the J theology of divine election, was deliberately rejecting another theological position which came to dominate Israel's literature between the two strands, though this theology is not found in Genesis 1–11.

This alternative theology was probably introduced into the J source after the fall of Samaria to the Assyrians in 721 BC, when following the warning of the eighth-century prophets Amos, Hosea and Isaiah, the northern kingdom of Israel disappeared for ever. This disaster caused Hezekiah of Judah to institute a sweeping reform (2 Kings 18) before, as Micah and Isaiah threatened, southern Judah suffered the same fate. This resulted in a revision of J which not only took account of the theological ideas of the northern kingdom, but also had to come to terms with its loss. As a result, Israel's election was no longer interpreted as absolute but conditional. At Sinai, Yahweh was understood not merely to have given Israel her law, but to have entered into a covenant (*berith*) with her which contained within it the threat of absolute rejection for disobedience of that law (Exodus 19:3–8, 24:3–8). This resulted in a substantial rewriting of the Sinai narrative (Exodus 19–24, 32–34).

Half a century later Josiah carried out a further and even more far-reaching reform (2 Kings 23) based on this theological assessment, which resulted in the centralization of all worship at Jerusalem. But this was to no avail. In 597 BC Jerusalem fell to the Babylonians and the leading citizens including King Jehoiachin were exiled in Babylon (2 Kings 24). Eleven years later (586 BC), after Zedekiah's rebellion, the Babylonians again took Jerusalem, and this time even the temple was

6

destroyed (2 Kings 25). These disasters led to the production of a new literary work which reached its final form sometime between 560 and 540 BC. In this the reform carried out by Josiah and reflected in the laws in Deuteronomy 12–26 was used to judge the faithfulness of Israel and her leaders, from the conquest to the exile. Scholars have therefore called this composition the Deuteronomic Work. It includes Deuteronomy, Joshua, Judges, 1 and 2 Samuel and 1 and 2 Kings, and is dominated by the covenant idea, namely that failure to obey Yahweh's law requiring exclusive allegiance to him inevitably leads to divine rejection. So in the climax of this Work, the Deuteronomic theologians record that the southern kingdom of Judah took no notice of the fall of the apostate northern kingdom of Israel to Assyria (2 Kings 17), but continued her apostate ways particularly in performing practices of Canaanite religion abhorrent to Yahweh. As a result Yahweh had no alternative but to implement the threat contained in the covenant theology and so revoke Israel's election. Yet the Deuteronomists recognized that Yahweh could if he wanted re-elect Israel and restore her to her land. Indeed they appear to have interpreted Jehoiachin's release from prison in Babylon in 561 BC (2 Kings 25:27–30) as a sign that he would do so.

So at the time that the second literary strand found in Genesis 1–11 was written, Israel's theology was dominated by the 'threat theology' used as the basis of the Deuteronomic Work. While this theology acknowledged the undeserved nature of Yahweh's election of Israel, it understood that election as conditional on obedience to his law as set out in Deuteronomy. Israel was then always under the threat of extinction, and such a threat would continue to be exercised even if God restored her and gave her a second chance. But for the author of the second literary strand in Genesis 1–11 such an understanding of God's nature was radically defective. Grace could never be conditional.

(v)

The second literary stage

This new author is called by scholars the Priestly Writer, and his work P, because of its dominant interest in cultic and ritual rules of priestly observance. While it is generally agreed that P was composed in

Babylon, its date remains uncertain. But because its theology is very close to that of the exilic prophets Ezekiel and the author we call Second Isaiah (Isaiah 40–55), it is probable that it comes from a similar time, and certainly not much after the exiles began to return to Palestine (538 BC). However it should not be assumed that all the stories, traditions, and regulations in P are late. Much ancient material is preserved. But what P does is to reassess Israel's theological position. While the author follows the plan of the revision of J following Hezekiah's reform, the effect of the incorporation of so much new P material into that revision was to make it totally subservient to P's theology. Nowhere is this clearer than in Genesis 1–11 itself.

Passages in Genesis 1–11 normally accredited to P are Genesis 1:1–2:4a, 5, 6:9–9:17 (though some J material is found here), 9:28–29, 10:1–7, 20–27, 31–32, 11:10–26, 27, 31–32. Apart from a new creation account, and the considerable supplementary material to the J narrative of the flood, these passages are concerned with genealogies which are so characteristic of P. For the whole work, which includes the books of Genesis, Exodus, Leviticus and Numbers, has a very precise chronology. Into this scheme Israel's history from the creation of the world to the death of Moses, now found at the end of Deuteronomy (34:1a,7–9) but which once concluded Numbers, is carefully worked. Later, because of the desire to have all the material concerning Moses and the law in one literary work, Deuteronomy was detached from the Deuteronomic Work and joined to P, resulting in the necessary transfer of the death of Moses. So the Pentateuch came into being.

P's concern is with the reconstruction of the post-exilic community. Unlike the Deuteronomic theologians, he recognized that inevitably the law would be broken but saw in the cult with its practice of sacrifice and atonement, even for the nation as a whole (Leviticus 16), the means whereby the life of the community could continually be renewed and reformed. For him Israel was no longer to see herself as always under threat of extinction at God's hands, but rather as the elect people of God for all time. But Israel's election was due to no merit of her own: she owed her existence to Yahweh alone and not to any endeavour on her part. While individual membership of the community of Israel was determined by obedience to the law, that community's continued existence depended solely on Yahweh's gracious election (cp. Ezekiel 37).

8

For P then the Sinai events are not seen as the inauguration of the covenant relationship with a band of runaway Hebrew slaves by which Israel came into being, and whose continued existence depended on obedience to the law. Rather her relationship pre-exists the giving of that law and is independent of it, for it was inaugurated in creation. As we shall see, this explains why P has to preface his work with a second creation account (Gen. 1:1–2:4a). While individuals who broke the law in any substantial manner would have to be excluded from the cult community because their action threatened the purity of that cult, Israel herself, despite all appearances to the contrary, could exist for all time. The only threat to her relationship with Yahweh was lack of faith on her part. This explains why the Priestly Work ends before the conquest of Canaan. Like other exilic and post-exilic theology it is uncertain about the outcome. Although Israel's future is assured by God, it none the less depends on Israel appropriating it for herself. The outcome therefore rests with the exilic generation to whom P wrote. Will they have sufficient faith to maintain their allegiance to Yahweh? Whatever may be happening on the world stage, he has not forsaken and will not forsake them. So, like Ezekiel and Second Isaiah, P places the responsibility for the future firmly on the exiles themselves. The author is hesitant—but his purpose is to dispel hesitancy by asserting in the face of the alternative Deuteronomic 'threat theology' that not only will God not let Israel go, but that he cannot. His love cannot be limited by man's failure. For Christians the cross reaffirms this truth. But the onus remains on man to accept or refuse God's grace. Until he does chaos reigns and the kingdom cannot come in all its fullness: man cannot re-enter that ordered garden which was God's will for him.

It must now be clear that Genesis 1–11 can be understood only as a theological work. Its concern is to proclaim its authors' understanding of the nature of God, the nature of man and the nature of their relationship. But while they never understood their material as an historical or scientific account of creation and of man's early history in the narrow sense of giving a precise record of the course of events, the authors none the less saw themselves as writing history and reflecting their scientific ideas. For these theologians Israel's present position was the result of what had happened in creation and the events that followed, events in which God's hand was readily apparent at all points, for nothing was outside his control.

Should Genesis 1–11 be called 'myth'?

The stories in Genesis 1–11 are, however, often referred to as 'myth' and their close relationship to other ancient Near Eastern material cited. We shall refer to such material in our later discussion. But it has become increasingly clear that 'myth' is a very hazardous term. While in the popular mind it refers to something which is untrue, of no substance, entirely illusory, scholars themselves have been unable to agree on a satisfactory definition for the term. Indeed the word is a comparative newcomer to theology, having been introduced in the nineteenth century. But it has been used in so many disciplines in so many different ways and has led to so much misunderstanding and controversy that it might be better if theologians abandoned it, particularly as it has the effect of separating off Genesis 1–11 as somehow different in kind not only from the rest of Genesis-Numbers of which it is an integral part, but also of implying that it is less 'historical' and therefore reliable than the accounts in say Samuel, Kings and Chronicles. But this both devalues Genesis 1–11 and overvalues the so-called historical books. In fact, whatever its source, all Old Testament material has been theologized—that is, its primary concern is with the faith of Israel and her understanding of the God who had elected her, and who from creation onwards had revealed himself in history. This even applies to the collections of laws found in Exodus, Leviticus and Deuteronomy. In essence, Genesis 1–11 is then no different from other Old Testament material, and should like the rest of the material be interpreted theologically.

Thus instead of categorizing the material as 'myth', theologians should concentrate on identifying those problems for which these stories were created as the answers. Indeed when we undertake this task in relation to Genesis 1–11 we shall find that the very same issues confront us. The stories then must be seen as literature designed to express the theological understanding of a particular people, though, as we shall see, they were quite prepared to draw on stories from other peoples which they then made their own. Hebrew literature must be allowed to speak for itself, rather than have imposed upon it categories and forms—myth, legend, saga—which can only distort and deceive. And when this is done, then the modern heresy that the writers of the Old Testament held only primitive religious ideas now dispelled by scientific twentieth-century man 'come of age', is itself

10

dispelled. For it is a complete delusion to imagine that the ancient Israelites could not have had a true vision of the transcendent God with whom they and we have to deal. Of course there are differences in outlook between the men of ancient Israel and the men of our modern world. It would be sheer foolishness to pretend otherwise. But while science has undoubtedly expanded man's knowledge, and therefore his ability to understand his material world, it has not affected his ability to think and experience for himself. There is therefore no *prima facie* reason why the insights of the ancients into the mystery of God and the equally perplexing mystery of man could not in fact speak to our present condition.

No doubt there are many different ways in which we could examine the material. We could certainly attempt to do this chronologically, taking the J passages first and then the P ones. But since in my view P took over J and clearly regarded this material as integral to his own theological standpoint, I propose to take the material in the order in which we have it, seeing it as a whole. So let us take the advice of the king in *Alice's Adventures in Wonderland* and begin at the beginning and go on till we come to the end: then stop.

Chapter 2

The Seven-Day Creation Story (Gen. 1:1–2:4a)

(i)

Did anything exist before creation?

Paradoxically the very first verse of the Hebrew scriptures poses considerable difficulties in translation. This reminds us that the Old Testament is written in an ancient language, classical Hebrew, and that it is not always clear what any particular word or passage means. Here the problem is whether we are to understand that there already existed a formless waste and primaeval sea out of which God created the world, or whether the Priestly Writer held that nothing pre-existed God's action. If we take the latter view then we translate, like the Authorised Version, Revised Version, Revised Standard Version and Jerusalem Bible: 'In the beginning God created the heavens and the earth'. This is the doctrine of creation out of nothing (*creatio ex nihilo*). But comparison with the Babylonian creation epic *Enuma Elish*, probably dating from the early part of the second millennium BC, supports the translation of the New English Bible which sees verse 1 as a temporal clause and verse 2 as describing the situation which existed before God started his activity: 'In the beginning of creation, when God made heaven and earth, the earth was without form and void, with darkness over the face of the abyss'.

Now it seems clear that while the Priestly Writer was certainly aware of Babylonian theology, his intention was to make a sharp distinction between their heathen ideas and his own. For in the aftermath of the Babylonian conquest, there were plenty of Jews who were tempted to adopt the apparently more sophisticated Babylonian religion whose validity seemed confirmed by the material success of the conquest.

The Babylonian creation epic begins by describing the chaos-waters which existed before creation, and then goes on to recite at considerable length the birth of the gods and their various conflicts leading to the eventual creation of the heavens and the earth out of the body of the defeated sea goddess Tiamat. Finally man is created. Yet in the P account hardly any of these Babylonian ideas survive. The account itself, in accordance with current Jewish theology, is strictly monotheistic. There is only one God who alone is responsible for creation. It is due to his command that creation takes place. This is the first act in history which he alone controls. The Priestly creation account thus removes all mention of the conflict between the gods, traces of which are found elsewhere in the Old Testament (Psalm 74:13–15, 89:10; Isaiah 51:9–10), and replaces it by a measured series of events by which the world as we know it comes into being. In view of this deliberate re-presentation of the creation story, it seems preferable to take verse 1 as a summary statement formally establishing the theological principle of *creatio ex nihilo* as in the older versions of the Bible. All matter is thus held to be dependent on God alone and does not pre-exist his creative activity. Verse 1 thus asserts the essential freedom of God, his utter transcedence. His power over the created world is absolute.

We have then to ask why reference is still made in verse 2 to the formless waste and primaeval sea. Indeed some scholars have identified the Hebrew word for the latter, *tehom*, with the Babylonian sea goddess Tiamat. Certainly this mention of water is foreign to arid Palestine (cp. Gen. 2:4b–6) and reflects a Babylonian origin.

The answer is that although the Priestly Writer wished to expunge all reference to Babylonian ideas of a primaeval conflict from his account, he none the less believed that the alternative to God's creation was not non-existence, but lifeless emptiness amid the watery chaos. Thus creation was always subject to the possibility of a return to that formless void which was its 'natural' state. By preserving this reference to primaeval chaos from the Babylonian account, the Priestly Writer skilfully shows that God's creation cannot be taken for granted. It will not endure willy-nilly, but needs man to order it. But in contrast to the Babylonian account, the Priestly Writer pictures the formless waste and primaeval sea in entirely passive terms. There is no force within them which is opposed to God and consequently no idea of conquest over them on his part. They merely represent what will be creation's fate if man fails in God's commission to him. This chaos was what awaited the disobedient generation of the flood (Gen. 6–8), whom P identified with those responsible for the exilic situation in which those to whom he wrote now were.

Over the formless waste and primaeval sea the wind of God moved. But this wind is no ordinary wind, for it is God's creative power which takes hold of men and matter and transforms them from their natural state. It is none other than God's Spirit (Job 33:4). So through the working of his Spirit the natural emptiness of the world gives way to the ordered creation that God wills, just as for Christians 'natural' man also becomes a different creature through the gift of the Spirit in baptism—'born again'. The Hebrew word describing the activity of the Spirit is also used in Deuteronomy 32:11 of an eagle trying to get her young to fly. Like the mother bird, the Spirit of God stirs up what is inactive to fulfil its true potential. With the Spirit's presence both man and matter become what they have it in them to become. For the Christian, like the young bird, the Spirit stirs him to 'take off'. Without the Spirit, as with creation itself, he is a formless waste, a chaotic being.

(ii)

Why a seven-day creation account?

We have already indicated that the theology of the Priestly Writer was distinctive from that of Babylon. Indeed it seems probable that he took over an existing Babylonian eight-day creation account, and by squashing two events into each of the third and sixth days, succeeded in completing creation before the seventh day on which he pictures God resting. Thus in his account the sabbath became part of the creative process itself. There never was a time when it did not exist.

The actual origin of the sabbath is not entirely clear. Although etymologically it is now connected with the verb to rest, its proper meaning is probably 'stopping day', that is a day which divides one block of days off from another. We know that there were similar stopping days in Babylon, and attempts have been made to find the origin of the sabbath there. But there is no record anywhere outside Israel of a regular stopping day every seventh day. In view of this, it seems best to see the sabbath as a Hebrew institution. It certainly pre-existed the exile (2 Kings 4:23; Isaiah 1:13; Hosea 2:13; Amos 8:5) and its observance is, of course, enjoined by the fourth commandment (Exodus 20:8–11), and other pre-exilic law (Exodus 23:12, 34:21). Indeed its institution may go back to the time of the exodus and symbolize in the break from regular daily toil the Hebrews' freedom from foreign political control. They were no longer Pharaoh's slaves to be ordered about by the Egyptians, but free men who could control their own working lives. Certainly throughout the Old Testament period, and even in the time of Jesus, the sabbath in spite of increased restrictions remained a day of joy.

14

But the Priestly Writer takes the inauguration of the sabbath back from Sinai to the beginning of history itself. Thus in contrast to the Deuteronomic version of the Decalogue (Deut. 5:15), where sabbath observance is connected with deliverance from Egypt, in the Exodus version (Ex. 20:11), now part of the Priestly Work, the sabbath is related to creation. But since the only people in the world who kept the sabbath were the Jews, this indicated that they too must have been in God's mind at creation. Their history does not begin with the exodus from Egypt, not even with the call of Abraham. It began at creation in which they too form part of the ordered fabric brought about by the seven days of God's activity. In other words, like sun and moon, earth and sea, animals and man, the Jews are integral to God's order, immutably fixed. If they ceased to exist it would be as if the moon ceased to exist: both are unthinkable.

Now it is apparent why P had to provide a new creation account to preface his whole literary work. By making the sabbath the climax of creation, he proclaimed to the disillusioned Jews in exile that no matter what appearances to the contrary might be, their place in the world was assured. Unlike any other race, they were in God's mind at creation: as long as that existed, they would exist too. Although as a result of the Babylonian conquest the Jews no longer constituted an independent nation, their status in God's plan for his world was in no way affected by their political fate. They were the chosen and nothing could cancel their election. The Deuteronomic theology had been wrong to think that Israel's fate was ultimately determined by obedience to her law: God's grace could not be so limited. She must endure punishment for her disobedience: indeed in P's view the exile was entirely caused by failure to keep the sabbath. But the very sabbath itself confirmed her position, which only lack of faith on Israel's part could throw into doubt. That is why the Priestly Writer thought that the breaking of the sabbath was such a heinous offence. Together with circumcision (Gen. 17), observance of the sabbath alone constituted in heathen Babylon the distinguishing marks of those faithful Jews unwilling to apostatize, and who in P's theology ultimately held all men's fate in their hands.

This theme of Israel's unconditional election has now been taken over by the Christian church through its claim to be the true Israel. Consequently there is no place for pessimism in Christianity. No matter what conditions confront them, Christians can only exercise present faith and future hope.

How did the Priestly Writer understand the created world?

While the borrowing of existing material makes clear that the Priestly Writer was not primarily writing a scientific account of creation, but rather seeking to assert the theological truth that this was due not to accident but to God's deliberate action, none the less his account reflects the scientific ideas of his time. Thus the earth is envisaged as a flat disk floating on the primaeval waters with over it the firmament, thought of as an inverted metal basin, beyond which lay the waters of the heavens. From here God sent rain, and from the waters below the earth came the sea, rivers and springs (Gen. 1:6–8). But the earth's existence was precarious: too much water could fall from the heavens or rise from under the earth and engulf it (Gen. 6–9). Indeed scholars have shown that the original purpose of the ancient Near Eastern creation accounts was to give threatened man security through their recitation in the cult.

In his seven-day scheme of creation, P is concerned to rule out all foreign religious ideas. So God not only creates all plant and animal life, but provides their means of propagation. This includes even man—created male and female—whose sexual functions far from being ignored or dismissed as a necessary evil to provide for the future of mankind, are not only taken for granted but expected to be luxuriated in. There is then no need for Israel to resort to fertility deities. Nor is God himself to be treated as such. In creation itself, in providing seed, seasons and semen, God had done all that was necessary. The division of plants into those such as cereals which scatter their seed, and those like grapes, figs and olives whose seed is hidden in its fruit, reflects current scientific observation (Gen. 1:11–12). Similarly animals are divided into appropriate categories (Gen. 1:24–25). Further, it is God who creates the astral bodies (Gen. 1:14–18), thereby indicating that they are in his control. They are not to be worshipped as was widely done in the ancient Near East, which explains the deliberate avoidance of naming the sun and moon (Gen. 1:16), nor held to have independent power to influence men's destinies. Similarly both the sea and sea monsters are God's handiwork and, as subject to him, no longer to be feared (Gen. 1:20–21).

Throughout Genesis 1 the products of God's activity are described as 'good'. This indicates the moral perfection of God's world in which

16

both animals and man are created as vegetarian. Only later (Gen. 9:3) was P to recognize the eating of meat as a 'necessary evil' (see pp. 48f.). By asserting the moral nature of creation, P dismisses the idea of an ultimate source of evil. Its entry into the world was subsequent to creation. The co-existence of ultimate good and ultimate evil (dualism) is thus ruled out. Again this is a cause for joy, for it indicates the complete sovereignty of God whose creative purpose of ensuring the good order cannot ultimately be thwarted—provided men have sufficient faith. This same idea is present in the messianic passage in Isaiah 11:6–9, which looks forward to the re-establishment of God's original order in creation.

This sovereignty of God is confirmed by the use of the Hebrew word *bara* (create) which is used in the Old Testament only of God's creative activity, and never presumes the existence of any material for that creation. But as its frequent use in Second Isaiah indicates (Isaiah 40–55), this creative activity is not simply for its own sake, but has as its ultimate purpose man's salvation. Genesis 1 is then for P the first episode in this historic process as well as reflecting the ultimate goal of the God who will not give up until it is secured. Thus in his account of creation, the Priestly Writer does not primarily set out to establish a doctrine of creation, but rather sees creation as an ancillary to the doctrines of election and salvation in which his contemporaries are invited to reaffirm their faith.

God achieves his creation through a series of commands. It is his word which effects what it signifies and does not return to him empty (Isaiah 55:11). This again indicates God's transcendence: he is beyond, other. But since it is through his word that he communicates with men, whether in revealing his will through his *torah* or in speaking directly to prophets and priests, God is no absentee landlord. He has not created his world and then left it to its own devices. While he has provided the means for its self-perpetuation, God is ever in dialogue with man in order that his creation may be as he intended it to be—good. But, as we shall see, in the end this depends on man's co-operation, for to man earthly sovereignty has been given (Gen. 1:26–28). And this is something which once given cannot be taken away. But if man fails to heed God's word, then the earth will return to that formless waste of lifeless emptiness where neither vegetation, animal nor man can survive (Jeremiah 4:23–26).

(iv)

What is the place of man in the Priestly account of creation?

In the Babylonian creation epic man is made out of the blood of a dead god, but P describes man as made like everything else at the direct order of God (Gen. 1:26–27). Yet some scholars have seen echoes of Babylonian theology in God's address to the heavenly realm: 'Let us make man in our image, after our likeness', for the plural form is frequently found in the Babylonian creation epic. But long before P wrote, Israel had adopted into her theology the idea of a heavenly court in which Yahweh presided over semi-divine beings (1 Kings 22:19–22; Psalm 82:1, 89:6–8; Isaiah 6:1ff.). Indeed this idea was already present in the J creation account (Gen. 3:22, 11:7). And despite his strict monotheism, P deliberately repeats it in Genesis 1. His purpose is to contrast his account of creation with the J story of man's expulsion from the garden where man is condemned for trying to make himself 'like one of us'—that is, break out of those limitations which constitute the true human state. But P's concern is to assert that in spite of man's repeated acts of arrogance towards God as set out by J (Gen. 3:22, 11:6), God has made man in the image of the *elohim*, the ordinary Hebrew word for God or gods. In other words man properly belongs in intimate relationship with the divine world. He was created both to hear and be heard by God—created to be his reflection in the world. But by the typically Hebrew double expression 'in our image, after our likeness' the Priestly Writer deliberately points to man's paradoxical position of both nearness to and yet distance from God. Although intimately and uniquely related to *elohim*, he is not one of the divine ones, and must remain distinct and separate within the earthly realm.

As a result of P's new theology there is in Genesis 1–11 a tension between man's intended status as 'like one of us' and his arrogance in making himself 'like one of us'. But in bringing out this tension, P has emphasized man's proper dignity. Unlike the animals he is given the power to communicate with the divine world and so engage in God's ordering activity. But just as a limit is set to the activities of the divine beings (Gen. 6:1–4), so also there is a limit to man's actions, a limit set by his residence on earth and not in the divine realm. None the less in contrast to the Babylonian creation epic, which sees man as created for the service of the gods, man is commanded to act as the representative

18

of the creator in his creation, to master and control it (Gen. 1:28). The Old Testament thus takes a positive view of scientific research and technological advancement. P uses royal language to delineate man's role. But man's kingship over creation is not to be one of exspoilation. His is to be a responsible government in which God's order is maintained. Nor is there any thought of any part of mankind dominating another. All men share the same given status and the same responsibility.

Although the Priestly Writer confirms Israel's election, he recognizes that, if God's original order is to be restored, then Israel must bring all men into that relationship for which they were created. This is why the blessing of all peoples in Abraham (Gen. 12:3) still remains the climax of Genesis 1–11 (see pp. 60f.). In this P was reflecting current theology as seen in Second Isaiah (49:6, 55:5), Trito-Isaiah (61:5–7), Zechariah (8:20–23) and Isaiah 11:10, which was later tacked on to the messianic prophecy of Isaiah 11:1–9. The importance of Genesis 1:1–2:4a is that, although it confirms in the most unlikely political situation the place of Israel in God's salvation plans, it also makes plain God's concern for all peoples, for all are made in the image of the *elohim*, and therefore none can be ignored. For such a theology to be proclaimed at the moment of apparent total failure is a startling testimony to faith: it was to find its echo on the cross.

Chapter 3

The Eden Creation Story (Gen. 2:4b–25)

(i)

How does J picture creation?

The most striking difference between the Priestly Writer's account of creation and the J story of Eden is that the latter is not really a creation story at all. As far as the heavens and the earth are concerned, all that J provides is an introductory statement (verse 4b). Rather the whole attention of J's narrative is focussed on the creation of man. The Priestly Writer has found it necessary to retain this story both because it confirms and supplements his own more abbreviated summary of man's creation, but also because it provides the setting for the story of man's attempt to become 'like one of us' (Gen. 3).

J pictures a world in which neither of the basic requisites for cultivation are present—rain and man. This arid desert reflects a Palestinian background and in contrast to the P creation account influenced by its Babylonian setting, sees water not as the enemy of creation but its necessary agent. Though monotheism was not part of J's theology, the author none the less places the whole responsibility for creation on Yahweh alone. He acts by himself and without reference to or need of any other god.

In order that the earth can bring forth vegetation which in its turn will sustain man, God causes a flood to rise up from beneath the earth and water its surface. This translation followed by the New English Bible is preferable to the 'mist' of the older English versions. Then like a potter shaping his work, God forms man from clay. Here J is repeating what had become a standard picture of the method of man's creation throughout the ancient Near East. The word *adam* = man, mankind, is in fact a pun on the Hebrew word for earth, *adamah*. Both words derive from a common root meaning redness—the colour of soil and skin. As is the case with every Hebrew pun, two ideas, in this case man and earth, are understood to be intimately related and exercise power over each other. So man tills the soil to live, yet in the end is buried in it. As we shall see this again illustrates man's essential nature—that in both life and death he is confined to the earth and cannot break into the divine realm.

20

Into his clay model God breathes vitality. Simple observation showed that without breath, the body lost its life force and that it then deteriorated until it disintegrated in the earth. But there is no idea of man having a separate soul as the Authorised Version implies. For the Hebrews man was created as a complete unity. He was therefore thought of as either entirely alive or entirely dead. After death man went down to Sheol—the pit of the Psalms—where he spent his time in a shadowy state of non-experience. Real life for the Hebrews was confined to the earth, where the dead man's personality went on in his children. Hence the hope for every Hebrew was that he would die 'full of days' leaving behind him many generations (Job 42:16–17).

(ii)

What is man's function?

Man is placed by God in a garden. This is located somewhere in the east where the whole of J's narrative takes place up to the call of Abraham. The east was particularly associated with wisdom. The garden is pictured as an oasis in a desert, an orchard of trees perfectly ordered and abundantly stocked with fruit. Two trees are specifically named, the tree of life and the tree of the knowledge of good and evil (verse 9). In Hebrew thought the latter does not refer to moral questions but rather is a comprehensive phrase indicating knowledge of everything—the kind of knowledge that only God can have, and which is therefore forbidden to man.

It is clear that more than one ancient story lies behind Genesis 2–3, and scholars have often tried to divide up the chapters into literary units. But in fact J has so woven the material together that this is no longer possible. Further it destroys his purpose. Both the question of immortality and the question of the kind of knowledge which men can have concern him, though it is the latter which now dominates his narrative.

The garden is variously described as in Eden (verse 8), of Eden (verse 15), and in verse 10 a river flows out of Eden to water it. Clearly J's purpose, if somewhat vaguely expressed—and this may have been intentional—was to give Eden (= delight) a precise geographical location. Here 'history' began—though J would never have expected anyone to mount an expedition to find its site. Indeed we cannot now be certain where J imagined his oasis to be, for the identity of some of the rivers and the lands they flowed round cannot be ascertained (verses 10–14). Probably J was picturing the rivers encompassing the whole earth, and as in Ezekiel 47, saw their waters as a source of blessing for all lands. Certainly there were other ancient traditions associated with Eden which are not used by J (Ezekiel 28).

But man was not set in Eden to do nothing: he is specifically put there to till the garden and keep it, that is to maintain it as the perfect place it is (Gen. 2:15). While man was clearly meant to luxuriate in the garden, luxury does not consist in idleness but in labour which results in the maintenance of God's order. In doing this man fulfils himself. Thus there is no thought here of God dwelling in the garden. Though man can meet God there after work (Gen. 3:8), he is a visitor and not a resident. Indeed God's presence at a particular place and time can never be guaranteed, for it is up to him how, where and when he appears, for God is not man's to control. The maintenance of faith in the face of the absence of God is an important Old Testament theme (e.g. Psalms 10, 22; Job) and is at the heart of the passion narrative (Mark 15:34).

The garden then has been handed over to man as God's tenant, who like all lessees has to maintain it in the state in which he found it. But man has a choice as to whether he will do this or not. This freedom to decide is given him when God prohibits him from eating from the tree of the knowledge of good and evil—of rejecting his creaturely status. Man then is no robot: his co-operation with God is not guaranteed but is up to man himself. Although God lavishes on him a super-abundance of delights, he also gives him the opportunity to reject his providence. Free will is then inherent in man and indicates that to be human means to live with the tension of temptation ever present. Not even Jesus could avoid that. But it also shows that God has made man for a real relationship in which man is given the opportunity of the joy of response to God. But as P indicates by adopting and reaffirming J's theology of grace, paradoxically it is man who is more free than God: for while man is given the choice of obedience or not, God cannot let man go. Despite man's rejection, God ever seeks him—a seeking which the Old Testament describes as starting with the dawn of time, and which for Christians reaches its culmination in the incarnation, crucifixion and resurrection of Jesus Christ.

(iii)

What is the place of woman in the J account?

In the Priestly Work man is created male and female and his sexuality taken for granted (Gen. 1:27). It is the God-given means of reproduction. P has no need to say more in view of the J account of the creation of woman. This begins with the recognition that man on his own is incomplete. So using the same material as for man (Gen. 2:19, cp. 7:22), God creates the animals to see if the requisite companion can be found. These are brought to man for naming, indicating his dominion over them. Here we see reflected J's wisdom background in the establishment of a recognized order to the animal world. Indeed Solomon himself was said to have excelled in such matters, being able to specify every variety of plant and beast (1 Kings 4:33f.). But in spite of man's basic affinity with the animals as a creature of earth, no suitable partner is found for him. Thus the author rules out any thought of sexual union between the human and animal worlds. In this J may be reflecting current abhorrence at such practices in the contemporary Canaanite cult designed to effect union between the worshipper and his god through a sacral animal which was subsequently sacrificed. It is then no accident that with the probable exception of adultery, the only sexual law as old as the united monarchy specifically prohibits bestiality (Exodus 22:19).

Finally with man's own rib, God creates woman, and man finds himself at last complete (Gen. 2:21–22). It has been suggested that God's choice of the rib explains why the rib cage only covers the upper part of the body, leaving the lower free for sexual intercourse. But if this is so, J makes no use of such an idea. Instead in man's poetic outburst at the sight of woman he again resorts to a pun, for the word for woman, *ishshah* is interpreted as a play on *ish,* man, though in fact these words have no etymological connection (Gen. 2:23). In this way J indicates the deep relationship between the two and their mutual power over each other.

Man's enjoyment of Eden is now total for he can be what he was made to be through the sexual fulfilment of his nature which had hitherto no opportunity for expression. As with all else in Eden, he is expected to luxuriate in this gift (cp. the Song of Songs). Further J points out that it is this sexual attraction of male and female which explains how a man may rightly sever himself from that other natural relationship which he has hitherto enjoyed—parental love (Gen.

23

2:24). And J concludes his account by noting that man and woman's joy was so complete that it knew no inhibitions (Gen. 2:25).

For J then marriage was man's natural state. While his account is clearly written from a male standpoint, and is unconcerned with such issues as polygamy, which was not prohibited in biblical times, his intention is to affirm that there is a timeless natural order of human relationships which God has ordained and wills everyman to enjoy.

The importance of Genesis 2 cannot be recognized until Genesis 3 has been read. J's purpose is not to speculate on the origin of the world or even on the origin of man. Thus he is not concerned with the question whether man descended from a single pair (monogenism) or from multiple origins at various points in the world (polygenism). Rather his purpose in this introduction to the acount of man's disobedience is to establish quite unequivocably that evil had no part in God's creation. Its entry into the world was subsequent to that world's creation. In asserting this, the J account is in marked contrast to the Babylonian creation epic in which evil is recognized as having existed from the beginning, and whose power neither the gods nor man can escape.

Chapter 4

Expulsion from Eden (Gen. 3)

(i)

What is the function of the snake?

The snake plays a prominent role in the literature and cults of the ancient world, echoes of which are found in Israel's religion (Numbers 21:9; 2 Kings 18:4). Of all creatures it was the most mysterious both in its movement (Proverbs 30:19) and apparent ability to prolong its life through casting its skin. This may explain its connection with stories concerning immortality. But there is no thought of this in Genesis 3; nor is the snake to be understood as Satan or the Devil. It is described quite simply as the craftiest of the creatures which God has made. In this way J delineates the other boundary within which discussion of the origin of evil must take place. In Genesis 2 he had asserted that God was not responsible for the origin of evil: but in Genesis 3, in locating the source of evil in the snake, one of his creatures, J indicates that even evil is in God's control. Thus as in the P account of creation, any separate independent source of evil is ruled out (dualism). But having stated God's relationship to evil, J is no longer interested in explaining its origin. Instead he concentrates on the fact of evil, and its consequences for man confronted by it.

The snake confirms his reputation by asking the woman a question which cannot be directly answered (Gen. 3:1), and so leads her to start off on the wrong foot. Having isolated her vulnerability, he induces her to doubt God. Had God in fact denied *adam* his proper status as like the *elohim?* The woman succumbs to the temptation to grasp at divinity, and in doing so, she and her husband discover their essential creatureliness in a way which was never apparent to them before (Gen. 3:7). While their action matures them in their understanding of what it means to be man, it does not allow them to find out anything outside the limits of their humanity.

By making him fall victim to the snake's craft, J holds man responsible for his failure, a responsibility man readily recognizes in his own guilt and which requires God's punishment. But while man had a free choice as to whether he would succumb to the snake, he had no freedom to avoid that choice which is thrust upon him. And in the way in which J presents the story there is an inevitability about man's failure. Whether he likes it or not, it is part of man's nature to try and be like the *elohim*. Though he is responsible for his actions, yet he is determined by his circumstances, his separation from the heavenly realm. For J free will and determinism are not contradictory concepts. So *adam* has to recognize both if he is to understand his nature. But man's failure does nothing to alter his created form. As we saw in Genesis 2 (p. 22), the capacity for disobedience was present in man from the time he was placed in Eden. The result then of his action is not that he becomes different—but that his situation becomes different. He no longer enjoys Eden.

It is then a mistake to talk here about 'the Fall' or 'original sin' in the sense that man is no longer constituted as God created him. This is a Christian doctrine based on St Paul's letter to the Romans (5:12–21) where the apostle uses late Jewish speculation on the effect of man's sin in Eden (cp. 2 Esdras 7:118; Ecclesiasticus 25:24; Wisdom 2:23f.). It has no part in Old Testament theology. In this sin is not understood as a flaw in man, but as something which presents itself to him from outside his self and to which he may assent, but from which he can be forgiven (Ezekiel 18). Thus while the Psalmist sees the hopelessness of the situation into which he has been born, and which must inevitably corrupt him, yet he knows that God can utterly free him from all stain (Psalm 51). J is then not concerned with how the tendency to commit sin is passed on—certainly not in tracing it to the sexual act—but rather to recognize that this tendency is the common experience of *adam* in every generation. While the snake indicates that the power of evil lies outside man, the story points to that power inevitably finding its expression through man's desire to be 'like one of us'. Man is thus called to live with the tension of the reality of evil for which he is not responsible (the snake), but which he cannot avoid because he will not accept the limitations of his humanity. Only Jesus did that, which is why he remained sinless. He alone was perfectly man.

The snake then is J's literary device whereby he is able to do justice both to God and man. By attributing the original temptation to the snake, the author tells us nothing about the mystery of the origin of evil. That is part of the knowledge of the *elohim* which man cannot have. But the snake indicates that while evil is a fact outside man's control, it is within God's. It is often said that Genesis 3 plays no further part in the Old Testament. In a sense this is true: but the reason is that the rest of the Old Testament is to be understood in its light. In the first composition of the Hebrew scriptures, J established the

26

predicament of man in the world in which God has set him: no one later saw fit to quarrel with his diagnosis.

(ii)

What is the nature of God's judgement?

The man and the woman hide from God because they no longer feel themselves fit to be in his presence (Gen. 3:8). This is always the result of sin, for it reminds man of the distance which separates him from God. Nakedness was considered highly improper in Israel, being connected with the cultic rites of Canaanite religion (2 Samuel 6). So J uses his story not merely to explain why men wear clothes, but why they should do so. Further these clothes are now provided by God himself (Gen. 3:21). Thereby J asserts his theology of grace, that even though man rebels against him, God will seek him out for he accepts him as he is. In other words while man's sin does nothing to change his essential nature as created by God, neither does it alter God's nature. Though man's situation is no longer Eden, none the less what was true of God's relationship with man in Eden remains true after his expulsion. Neither man's sovereignty within creation, nor his commission to order it is withdrawn.

But before God confirms his desire for man, J uses the story of man's disobedience to explain a number of the more unpleasant facts of life—both for snakes and man (Gen. 3:14–19). All of these involve the struggle for survival. Thus unlike other animals, the snake is deprived of legs and in order to move must wriggle on its belly, clearly imagined as a painful process. Further it is limited to a diet of dust—another faulty observation of contemporary science. In addition perpetual war is ordained between the snake and man, with each set on destroying the other. For woman the joy of childbearing is now to be accompanied by pain and suffering. And man, created to cultivate the ground, can only do so with considerable personal effort and with only partial success. The effect of his seeking to be like *elohim* is that the whole created order suffers. As part of creation, man cannot act independently of it. It is only now that the full implications of J's theological insight are being properly recognized in the clear interaction of man and his environment and man and his body.

27

So J concludes his curses by reminding man of the most unpleasant fact of his creaturely status—death. This is not part of his punishment, but his natural destiny. For nowhere in the J account is there any suggestion that man was originally intended to be immortal (cp. Ecclesiasticus 25:24; Wisdom 2:23f.). Death should however serve to remind him that no matter how hard he tries he cannot in the end 'be like one of us': *adam* is of *adamah*, and to the earth he must return (see p. 20).

The naming of Eve, 'mother of all living', properly belongs with the birth of the first child in Genesis 4, for it presupposes that the woman has already borne children. But after the reference to death, it has been found necessary to affirm that the blessing of procreation given at creation remains valid. The naming is then an act of faith—man's reacceptance of his role in God's scheme of things despite all the hardships which he now faces. For in spite of man's disobedience and God's quite justified punishment, God and man remain on the same side, committed to thwarting evil (which is located outside both of them) in the proper ordering of creation. Indeed without man, God cannot achieve this purpose.

(iii)

Why does the tree of life conclude the narrative?

So far the tree of life has only been mentioned once, as a central feature of the garden in Genesis 2:9. Now it reappears in the story as the reason for man's expulsion from Eden (Gen. 3:22). Long before J wrote, more than one story circulated in the ancient Near East telling how man was destined for immortality, but was cheated out of it. So in the Epic of Gilgamesh, Gilgamesh obtains a herb which has the power of renewing life only to have it stolen by a snake when bathing. And in the Myth of Adapa the hero due to false advice refuses the bread and water of immortality and so is tricked out of it. But in contrast J's fear is that man may grasp something to which he is not entitled. Immortality, like the knowledge of good and evil, was reserved for the *elohim*. So God addresses the heavenly beings. Since man has already attempted to become 'like one of us' by trying to gain that knowledge which only the *elohim* could have, so he must be prevented from eating of the tree of life and grasping that other distinguishing mark of

28

divinity over against humanity—immortality. Consequently man is expelled from the garden and a heavenly being is posted to guard it (Gen. 3:23–24). It is probable that in the reign of Solomon the cherubim became part of Israelite religious symbolism, the ark being placed under representations of these winged semi-divine creatures for protection (1 Kings 8:6–7).

So man goes out from Eden to do that for which he was created, no longer in the ordered existence of the garden but in the conflict situation of a marred creation. But the Eden story indicates that though his grasping at divinity must result in punishment, God will not cast him off. Even though he eats from the tree of the knowledge of good and evil, he does not die. In this the snake was right, though this does not mean that man and the created order can escape the consequences of his action. But despite his disobedience, *adam* continues to remain the object of God's care and protection, for in the end only through him can God's plan for his creation be realized. So Genesis 2–3 asserts not only the essential separation of *elohim* and *adam*, but also their necessary inter-dependence ever to be secured through God's grace alone.

Finally we may note that throughout Genesis 2–3 there has been no need to understand *adam* as a proper name. J is not concerned with a particular individual in a particular place at a particular time, but with the timeless tension of what it means to be man. Although scientific study—including the social sciences—would question many of J's presuppositions which reflect the thought-forms and customs of his day seen for instance in his understanding of the place of women in marriage (Gen. 3:16), yet his analysis of human nature remains uncomfortably true. But as P confirms, it is a matter of faith whether one accepts the full implications of this analysis—that man is no animal but made 'like one of us', yet remains part of creation and so cannot by his own efforts become 'like one of us'. It seems an apparent contradiction, but only through its acceptance can man be truly man.

Chapter 5

The Story of Cain (Gen. 4)

(i)

Why does J tell the story of Cain and Abel?

Scholars have indicated that many ancient traditions underlie this narrative, but as in Genesis 2–3, J has so stamped his own theological purpose on the narrative that its varied background can no longer be discerned with any certainty. Nor does its identification matter for the understanding of Genesis 1–11. Most probably the original story had some connection with the Kenites, a tribe of wandering smiths, who had a close relationship with the Hebrews (cp. Judges 4:11); the Hebrew *qayin* can mean smith. But if so, this is now of no importance to J. Rather he uses it as a timeless illustration that once man has rebelled against God, then there is no longer any restraint on his actions against his fellow men. In other words J affirms the important theological truth neglected in our post-Christian humanistic age that man's only ultimate protection from man is the acknowledgement of God's sovereignty. Otherwise men will inevitably be consumed at worst by envy and jealousy, at best with righteous indignation, and take action to remedy what they consider wrong. Thus the Ten Commandments (Exodus 20; Deuteronomy 5), the foundation of all *torah* (law), regulate man's relations with both God and his neighbour. Man's nature being what it is, humanism as a creed remains an unrealistic ideal doomed to failure.

(ii)

Could Cain resist the sin demon?

That Genesis 4 is also the complement to Genesis 3 and must be interpreted alongside it, can be seen by the numerous literary parallels in which the tale is told. The setting no doubt reflects the agricultural society of J's own time with its shepherds and farmers sacrificing their thank-offerings. Certainly there is no attempt made to pretend that Cain and Abel are on their own. Indeed in order that Cain's action will be unobserved, he has to take Abel out into the uninhabited open country (Gen. 4:8).

As elsewhere J presents his material with strict economy. Both brothers offer sacrifices, but only Abel's is accepted. No reason is given why this should be so. We are certainly not to assume that Cain had done anything wrong, or that he only offered his sacrifice unwillingly. Like Abel, he clearly expected his offering to be accepted. When it was not, he was very angry. But Cain had no reason to be angry. God is free to act as he likes towards men. Nor does he have to provide a reason for his actions. Often his choices appear unexpected and even unfair. So God prefers Jacob to Esau, Joseph and David to their elder brothers. No one has a right over God. Indeed J readily recognized that in God's choice of the Hebrews, he had done the unexpected. The prosperity of Solomon's reign was not theirs by right, but solely due to his grace. To be angry at God's selection, is to seek to be like *elohim*—to presume to know how God should act. Life is unfair: people do not always seem to get their just deserts. But to be seized by envy or righteous anger, and take action against another to make things fair, is to presume to be *elohim*. Only God can know what is fair—or rather why things are as they are, fair or unfair.

The poetic Genesis 4:7 is difficult. It is usually interpreted as a challenge to Cain. If he does not fall victim to temptation, he will be acceptable to God. Although sin is waiting for him, yet he can resist it. In other words Cain has the freedom to choose.

But in fact it is probably better to understand verse 7 as a statement of the inevitability of Cain's failure. Once he had become angry he was doomed. This means that the last verb of the verse must be taken not in the active as in the Authorised Version or Revised Version, but in the passive as in the New English Bible. If this is so then we get a summary of *adam's* situation in Eden. The first line of verse 7 indicates that Cain is responsible for his actions, that is that he has free will. But the remainder of the verse asserts that in fact sin will master him, that is that the outcome is determined. Further by picturing sin as a demon at the door, J, as with the snake, locates the source of evil outside man. Just as *adam* in Eden was fated once the snake opened its mouth, even though he recognized his own responsibility for what had happened, so Cain cannot avoid failure, yet must be punished for his part in consenting to sin. Once more J pictures the tension of the human predicament—of having free will and yet being determined by circumstances. Man has a tendency to sin, to try to be 'like one of us', which mysteriously he cannot resist.

31

(iii)

Why does God protect Cain?

As with Genesis 3, as soon as the sin is committed, God is on the spot to interrogate the offender: 'Where is Abel your brother?' (Gen. 4:9). To understand the full irony of Cain's reply, it is necessary to know something about the Hebrews' idea of blood. They recognized that there were two ways in which men could die, either through loss of breath or blood. Since God gave men their vitality, both belonged to him. This is also true of animals. As we shall see, before eating meat, the blood of the animal had to be poured out into the earth and so back into God's possession (cp. Gen. 9:4). But when a man committed murder, he was understood to take possession of his victim's blood (2 Samuel 4:11). Literally this blood was on his hands—that is in his control, and God had to take action to recover it. So God is described as 'seeker of the blood' of the murdered man (Gen. 9:5, 42:22; Psalm 9:13; Ezekiel 3:18,20, 33:6,8). And this seeking is what God is doing when he appears before Cain. As he explains, Abel's blood has been crying to him to come and repossess it (Gen. 4:10). Cain's answer to God is then singularly ironic. He denies knowledge of his brother's whereabouts by claiming that it is no part of brotherly duty for him to 'shepherd' the shepherd (Gen. 4:9). But there is here a *double entendre*—by his action, Cain has in fact taken possession of Abel's blood, he *has* become his brother's keeper, and in so doing has in effect become 'like one of us', for blood belongs to God alone.

Further parallels with Genesis 3 appear. First the earth suffers as a result of Cain's act (Gen. 4:11–12). Man cannot divorce his activities from the effect they will have on the environment. And second, as J's readers knew, Cain, like *adam*, does not suffer the prescribed penalty of death. This was mandatory in the case of murder (Exodus 21:12), the execution being seen as a kind of sacrifice in which the blood of the murdered man was released to God. Instead of the death penalty, Cain, again like *adam*, is driven out—in Cain's case to fend for himself in an alien land. Excommunication was not a penalty of pre-exilic Israelite law, for, before the doctrine of monotheism arose after the exile, it was believed that if a person was expelled from Israel, he would be unable to know Yahweh, but would have to worship the gods of the foreign territory to which he was driven (cp. 1 Samuel 26:19f.). Even bad men were not to be allowed to do this. It is this

32

isolation from Yahweh which Cain fears (Gen. 4:13–14). By leaving the vicinity of Eden for a foreign land, he would be beyond God's reach. Anyone could kill him without the risk of Yahweh seeing it and taking vengeance to release his blood. But as God protects *adam* with clothes, so now he places a mark on Cain indicating his ownership (Gen. 4:16). Should anyone kill Cain, they knew they would have to reckon with Yahweh's vengeance, which, as J indicates by the use of the proverbial seven, will be unremitting (Gen. 4:15). So again we find that in the face of man's failure, God will not let him go. His grace cannot be curtailed. Though man must accept his responsibility for his failure and suffer punishment, God wills to know and be known by him. Man cannot put himself beyond God's love, no matter how hard he tries— even by crucifying his Son.

We can now see the repetitive nature of J's composition. This cyclic style is typically Hebrew (cp. Job and St John's Gospel). But as J continues to repeat himself, we shall see that his aim is to broaden the area of disobedience until all men throughout the world are involved. Then through one man, Abraham, the father of the Hebrews, J can start the reverse process whereby all can gradually be brought back into relationship with God (Gen. 12:1–3).

(iv)

What is the purpose of Cain's genealogy?

In this genealogy, which is independent of the Cain and Abel story, J draws on very ancient material. The family tree begins in Genesis 4:1, is broken off, and resumes again in Genesis 4:17. Attached to it, but originally independent, is the Song of Lamech which does refer to the Cain and Abel story (Gen. 4:23–24). Many of the names in this J genealogy appear again in the P genealogy in Genesis 5, some in a different form (see p. 36). These genealogies have been connected with the two Babylonian lists of semi-divine primaeval kings who reigned before the flood, but while there may be some truth in this as regards P, it is certainly not made clear here. Possibly the J genealogy was originally connected with the founding of the Kenite cities (1 Samuel 30:29), such a development being a considerable departure from the wandering life of this tribe of smiths. But if so, this connection is now entirely suppressed by J who again makes no

33

attempt to picture Cain as on his own. Questions about the identity of Cain's wife are therefore irrelevant.

J uses the genealogy to describe the gradual development of human civilization. Thus instead of the discovery of certain cultural gifts being traced back to the gods as in many religious traditions, J names the human ancestors who first developed these cultural activities (Gen. 4:21–22). Throughout there is a positive attitude to scientific, technological and social progress. But by attaching the Song of Lamech to the genealogy, J points out that paradoxically man's development is accompanied by a terrible escalation in violence.

In his Song, Lamech boasts of killing those who assault him and being prepared to undertake unimaginable revenge. As J's readers knew, there must be a murder for the death penalty to be exacted (Exodus 21:12,18–19). And that was inflicted by communal stoning after proper trial. For the civil offence of assault, damages were payable to the injured. J however pictures Lamech as a tyrant taking the law into his own hands and acting without any restraint. His purpose is to indicate that the advance of civilization both materially and socially—a good thing in itself—is vitiated through human arrogance in the exercise of indiscriminate violence by those who through such advance have gained power. J may well have been reflecting on the Solomonic era with its undreamt of wealth and cultural achievement won at the cost of considerable personal degradation and suffering leading eventually to the break-up of the empire (1 Kings 12). In any event he makes the important theological observation that human progress does not alter man's nature. It merely gives him the power to bring greater prosperity and greater suffering to more people. For J, the Song of Lamech marks another extension of man's rebellion against God.

J concludes by noting that from this primaeval time men called God by his proper Hebrew name, Yahweh (Gen. 4:26). This is in direct contrast to the other Old Testament tradition which, as we saw earlier (pp. 3f.), believed that this name was first disclosed to Moses prior to the exodus (Ex. 3:14), a tradition which P repeats (Ex. 6:3). The connection of the name Yahweh with Moses is probably historically correct, though its origin appears much older. But the explanation offered in Exodus 3:14 of its derivation from the verb 'to be' is a later interpretation of a word whose meaning was no longer understood. In contrast to the exodus tradition, J wanted to assert the universalistic nature of Yahwism. It was not a religion just for the Hebrews: it was

34

for all men, and according to J, had in primaeval times been so recognized. It was only due to the scattering of mankind (Gen. 11) that this was no longer true, though as God set about his salvation of the world, all nations would in the end find themselves blessed (Gen. 12:1–3). And in the establishment of the Davidic-Solomonic state incorporating so many people of different traditions and background, this was already coming about. For J, these citizens were all sons of Abraham, sharing a common heritage as heirs of God's promise, a heritage which was to be enjoyed by all mankind.

Chapter 6

The Generations from Adam to Noah (Gen. 5)

(i)

What is the purpose of Adam's genealogy?

Like J (Gen. 4:17–26), the Priestly Writer separates the stories of creation and the flood by means of a genealogy. While J continues the Cain narrative by beginning his genealogy with the birth of Enoch (Gen. 4:17), and afterwards provides Seth and Enosh with their own separate genealogy (Gen. 4:25–26), the Priestly Writer having summarized his creation account (Gen. 5:1–2) sets out in order the ten patriarchal generations from Adam to Noah combining the Cain and Seth genealogies (Gen. 5:3ff.). The names in J and P are virtually the same though P exchanges Mahalalel with Enoch who now comes seventh in his list.

J		P
(Gen. 4)		(Gen. 5)
Adam		Adam
	Seth	Seth
	Enosh	Enosh
Cain		Kenan
Enoch		Mahalalel
Irad		Jared
Mehujael		Enoch
Methushael		Methuselah
Lamech		Lamech
(for Noah see Gen. 5:29)		Noah

We have already noticed the existence of the two lists of semi-divine Babylonian kings who ruled before the flood (p. 33). While there is certainly no direct relationship between these lists and the P genealogy, it is probable that they influenced the Priestly Writer in the general construction of his narrative. So like the Babylonian lists, P meticulously records that each patriarch lived for an impossible number of years, though being mortals, these are measured in hundreds rather than the tens of thousands of the Babylonian lists. Curiously the biblical figures vary between the three ancient versions of Genesis—the Hebrew, Greek (Septuagint) and Samaritan—though the reason for this is unknown. No doubt the numbers, as so often in the Old Testament, were used as a kind of code, the key to which has not come down to us.

But the purpose of the genealogy is plain. It is P's equivalent of the Eden story. Like the loss of the idyllic conditions of the garden of delight, it indicates the consequence of sin. Although God of his grace was to rescue Noah and his family from the all-pervasive wickedness of the generation of the flood, man was never again to know that vitality measured in length of years for which God had destined him. The effect of his refusal to co-operate with God meant that both the duration of his ability to procreate and of life itself must be severely limited. But though the length of man's life is drastically curtailed, man still remains essentially the creature God intended him to be, made in his image and so able to know and be known by him. It is this likeness to God which Adam passes on to his son, Seth (Gen. 5:3). Again there is no thought here of the Christian doctrine of original sin. Man remains constituted as God intended him to be, sovereign over the created order which is his to control.

(ii)

What is the significance of Enoch?

With the exception of Enoch and the unfinished entry on Noah, the genealogy adopts a stereotyped pattern which records (i) the age of the patriarch at the birth of his first son; (ii) the number of the subsequent years of his life and the fact that he had other children; and (iii) his age at death, being the total of (i) and (ii).

However, P records that Enoch did not die but was 'taken' by God. We have already noted how the Priestly Writer changed J's order of patriarchs by placing Enoch in seventh place. In the Babylonian list of kings, the seventh was described as particularly favoured by the sun god, Shamash, and introduced to various mysteries by him. The fact that P gives Enoch, now in seventh position, a life-span of 365 years, particularly appropriate for a connection with the sun, can hardly be co-incidence, and confirms that P's alteration of J's order of patriarchs is deliberate. But as elsewhere in P, where Babylonian mythology is drawn on, it is only used to heighten P's own distinctive theological position, and in no way subjects Yahwism to foreign influence, but

D

rather serves to contrast Jewish monotheism with pagan ideas. For P it is 'walking' with the only God who created man that is important (Gen. 6:9).

The Enoch tradition was to have an enormous importance in the inter-testamental period when the apocryphal book of Enoch was composed (cp. Jude 14–15). But this early mention of the 'ascension' of Enoch (cp. Elijah in 2 Kings 2:1,9–11) indicates that the Enoch tradition is much older than the book that bears his name, though it was then, under the influence of Babylonian Jewry, that the mythological speculations associated with Babylonian theology became of such importance to Palestinian Jewish theology.

(iii)

What is the 'relief' which Noah will bring?

The P genealogy concludes with the birth of Noah, Lamech's death and the birth of Noah's sons (Gen. 5:28–32), at which point the genealogy breaks off to record the story of the flood. Into these verses constituted in the stereotyped P pattern verse 29 has been inserted. This belongs to J and offers an explanation of the meaning of the name Noah with a typical Hebrew pun. Just as Noah is to provide men with relief (*niham*) from working cursed ground which no longer co-operates with them (Gen. 3:17–18) by planting a vine (Gen. 9:20), so that vine will exercise control over him through his drunkenness (Gen. 9:21). But though wine can be abused, it is none the less seen as a divine blessing which alleviates the struggle of man's labour (cp. Psalm 104:15).

Chapter 7

The Story of the Flood (Gen. 6:1–9:17)

(i)

Was there a flood?

Stories of a colossal flood are widespread throughout the ancient world, not only in the ancient Near East, and considerable literature has survived. Of the Mesopotamian versions, the Babylonian Epic of Gilgamesh probably dating from the early part of the second millennium provides the closest parallel to the Genesis narrative. Like Noah, a man called Utnapishim receives prior notice of the impending disaster, builds a boat, and takes on board not only his family but representatives of all living creatures. After a terrible storm which results in a flood which covers even the tops of the mountains, his boat grounds on a peak. Like Noah again, Utnapishim having released birds to make certain that the flood is over, disembarks and sacrifices to the gods. But we must be careful of arguing that these similarities mean that the Genesis account is directly dependent on the Babylonian Epic of Gilgamesh. It is much more likely that both share a common tradition which the Hebrews inherited from Canaan after entry into that land. Further the stories are theologically totally dissimilar, one reflecting a crude polytheism, the other the absolute moral nature of the Hebrew God with whom alone Israel was to have contact.

Archaeological evidence is often cited as proof that there was a flood and excavations in the Tigris-Euphrates valley have indicated that it was subject to severe flooding in which specific cities were from time to time destroyed. But no evidence of a universal flood has ever been produced. Nor is it likely to be. For as with the Eden narrative, the authors are not concerned with history as such but with theology. This is true even of the Epic of Gilgamesh which concentrates on the question of man's mortality. The biblical authors use these ancient stories already applied theologically, to serve their own distinctive theological purposes. While the Epic of Gilgamesh pictures the gods in very human categories acting without any ethical basis, the biblical account concentrates on the theme already established in the Genesis narrative that while man's disobedience to God's will must result in immediate and inevitable judgement, that judgement none the less leads on to a further act of divine grace. The Genesis account thus exhibits no concern over man's mortality. That has already been accepted as part of what it means to be within the earthly realm in which God placed man and from which he cannot escape (Gen. 3:22–24). Rather the concern of the Genesis account is as always with the nature of man, the nature of God, and nature of the relationship which man can enjoy with God. In what sense can man know and be known by him?

(ii)

Who is responsible for the flood narrative?

We have already noted (p. 3) that like the creation stories, there appear to be two versions of the flood narrative. Besides numerous repetitions, this can be most clearly seen in the difference in the numbers and nature of the animals taken into the ark, and the nature and length of the flood. Many scholars hold that two independent narratives, J and P, have been later combined by a redactor. But since it is difficult to see the P narrative in Genesis 1–11 standing on its own without J, it is in my view more probable that P overwrote J, reworking and supplementing it with his own material and theological ideas. This better accounts for those passages where the language of J and P alternates not merely in blocks of material, but within one block itself, as in Genesis 7:6–23, and to a lesser extent in Genesis 8. But whichever view is taken, inconsistencies remain in the account of the flood as now presented, though they cause more difficulty to the modern reader with his analytical logical approach than to those for whom the scriptures were written as a continuing revelation of divine will in which God's word was constantly being reinterpreted and reactivated for successive generations in the changed conditions which confronted them. The flood narrative should not then be separated into sources and read as two different versions as is sometimes done, but taken as a whole. The Priestly Writer, with his own distinctive emphasis and in an entirely different historical situation, is reiterating J theology by directly using the J narrative as the framework for his own account.

(iii)

What is the function of the story of the Nephilim?

Genesis 6:1–4 acts as part of the prologue to the story of the flood. Originally this offered an explanation of the origin of a race of giants whom the Hebrews were said to have encountered on their entry into Canaan (Numbers 13:33; cp. Deuteronomy 1:28, 9:2; Joshua 15:14). These legendary monsters were held to be the offspring of the union of divine beings from the heavenly court with mortal women. This legend, which at first sight seems to have more in common with Greek mythology than Hebrew theology and caused considerable embarrassment to later Jewish and Christian theologians, owes its origin to Canaanite tradition. But it is now used by J to indicate the utter depravity that existed at the time of the flood. Disobedience had now spread to the heavenly court itself, with divine beings entering the earthly realm and confusing what must remain permanently separate. Here we have the reverse of man's attempt to acquire divine knowledge by eating of the fruit of the tree of knowledge of good and evil (Gen. 3) and of man's efforts to penetrate the divine realm through building a tower reaching into heaven (Gen. 11). But for J the divine and human realms are for ever distinct and movement between them prohibited not only for men, but also for the heavenly court. Accordingly, as in the stories of Eden and Babel, God immediately appears and passes sentence for this act of heavenly rebellion whose consequences are seen on earth. Some scholars have interpreted verse 3 which J has inserted into the original myth before verse 4 as a divine limit placed on man's life in contrast to the lengthy lives of the patriarchs (Gen. 5). But since J did not have P's genealogy before him and nowhere else in the Old Testament is the natural length of man's life thought of as one hundred and twenty years (cp. Psalm 90:10), this is improbable. Rather the verse refers specifically to the sentence passed on the monstrous offspring of these illicit divine/human relationships, and not on mankind in general. Their half-divine parentage has again raised the possibility that men could acquire the divine attribute of immortality. On the contrary, God affirms their mortality, and although they have his spirit within them, that will only enable them to survive one hundred and twenty years—that is less than double the normal life-span of seventy years.

J concludes his prologue to the flood narrative with a general comment on the state of mankind (Gen. 6:5–8). Once again evil is accepted as a fact and no explanation is offered for its origin. Unlike Gilgamesh where the flood results from divine petulance—the sudden increase in mankind with its consequent noise keeps the gods awake—in the Genesis narrative its infliction is ethically motivated. In unabashed anthropomorphic language derived from the intimacy of personal relationships so characteristic of Hebrew God-talk, J describes God as sorry that he had ever created man. Yet despite his wish to reverse the process of creation by obliterating both men, beasts, birds and reptiles, God cannot let man go. This is J's doctrine of grace, which, in the entirely different circumstances of the exile, P confirms. So through Noah, who in J's account is simply presented as finding favour in God's eyes, God plans a second start to creation, just as in the exilic situation he is to do so again by recreating a new Israel from the dead bones of the old (Ezekiel 37). Having made man in his own image to co-operate with him in the management of his world, God finds that he cannot do without him. But it is not man's righteousness which secures his position, but God's grace alone.

(iv)

What is significant in the P setting of the flood?

Genesis 6:9–22 acts as the Priestly Writer's introduction to the flood. Themes are here introduced which reappear in Genesis 9:8–17 which concludes his account. Relying on the J prologue (Gen. 6:1–8), the Priestly Writer introduces Noah who like Enoch (Gen. 5:24) walks with God. In contrast he describes all created matter, both man and beast, as utterly corrupt, and therefore as ready for divine destruction. Man's actions are again understood as affecting the whole created order.

The same Hebrew word is used in verses 11–12 to describe the corrupt state of all flesh as in verses 13 and 17 indicates its destruction—thus in typically Hebrew fashion making the punishment fit the crime. Those who ruin the created order which God had pronounced as good (Gen. 1:31) will themselves be ruined (cp. Psalm 53). This word again reappears in the conclusion of the flood narrative in Genesis 9:11, 15 where God promises Noah that he will never again destroy all flesh. Thus the Priestly Writer frames his account with the idea that while man and beast have corrupted their way—that is, gone against that moral order determined by God in creation—and must suffer the consequence of such action, yet such punishment is never to be repeated in such an absolute way. Though God is a moral God and must respond morally, his grace overrides his law. This is the message of both Old and New Testaments.

Clearly the Priestly Writer has in mind the generation of the exile. While their fathers had brought about the destruction of Jerusalem and the end of the old order (cp. Gen. 6:13), it is P's belief that God wills to re-create a new Israel which, despite the discontinuity brought about by the conquest of Jerusalem, destruction of the temple and exile in Babylon, yet is to be seen as the continuity of the old Israel whose election remains valid (cp. Isaiah 50:1). But this new Israel depends on the righteous appropriating what is theirs for the having. We have already recognized that this idea lies behind the seven-day creation account in Genesis 1:1–2:4a (pp. 14f.). It now dominates the flood narrative, which like the creation account, P has felt it necessary to overwrite.

So Noah acts as an example to the exilic age. As Ezekiel saw, no generation was in the end doomed because of its predecessor (Ezek. 18). It was still possible in spite of the chaotic events through which the exiles had lived to enjoy God's election as Noah by himself taking action had done (Ezek. 14:14,20). But this could only be achieved by positively accepting for oneself the good news which P proclaimed, that the elect people remained the elect people of God, even if the events by which their salvation would be achieved could not yet be seen. It is this idea which the writer of the Letter to the Hebrews takes up in citing Noah among the ancient heroes who acted by faith alone (Heb. 11:7).

The flood narrative no longer preserves J's description of the vessel which we call 'ark' from the Latin rendering *arca*. The word *tebah* used by P only appears elsewhere of the reed basket in which the infant Moses was placed (Exodus 2:3). But such reed vessels are still found in the Middle East and their sea-worthiness has been proved by modern voyages such as those of Thor Heyerdahl. Precise measurements are given for the construction of Noah's vessel, but these are not always easy to interpret. But it seems that P's vessel had one notable difference from J's: it had a window (cp. Gen. 6:16).

Genesis 6:17 introduces the Priestly Writer's concept of the flood as a return to that primaeval chaos which existed before creation. He uses the word *mabbul* only found in Psalm 29:10, an ancient Psalm taken over from the Canaanites in which Yahweh (formerly Baal) is pictured as enthroned as sovereign ruler over the primaeval waters of chaos. Confirmation of this cosmic interpretation of the flood is found in Genesis 7:11 where P describes the collapse of the created order in terms of the waters bursting up from beneath the earth and pouring down from above the firmament, the very reversal of that separation which God had achieved in the P creation account (Gen. 1:6–8). Yet there is no suggestion that these forces have any independent power of their own. It is through God's action alone that this reversal of his creation takes place.

It is at this point (Gen. 6:18) that another idea taken up in the conclusion of the flood narrative in Genesis 9:8–17 is introduced, the covenant (*berith*). No concept is more important in the Bible, for it is this word wrongly translated which has given us the titles Old and New Testament. Once more then P anticipates at the beginning of his story the eventual outcome of the events which he then goes on to describe, and which we shall consider when we reach the climax of his flood narrative (Gen. 9:8–17). But even before the flood takes place, in typically P style, we know that the story will have a happy ending, for God will bring Noah safely through it to a new relationship called a covenant. The same new relationship awaited the exilic generation for whom P wrote if only they would accept it.

Having made the vessel in which he is to ride out the flood, Noah embarks with his family and pairs of every animal, bird and reptile to ensure the survival of all species which God had made. Fish (Gen. 1:26), not being land creatures (Gen. 1:24), are left to swim it out! Since both men and animals are thought of as vegetarian (Gen. 1:29–30), no problems arise over accommodating so many different species on one boat, and food is taken on board for survival. P concludes this section of his narrative by noting Noah's complete obedience.

(v)

What is significant in the J setting of the flood?

Genesis 7:1–5 preserves the J command to Noah to embark. In contrast to the P account, J lays down that the vessel should be filled with seven pairs of clean animals and one pair of unclean (Gen. 7:2). The reason for this becomes clear in the climax of the J flood narrative (Gen. 8:20–22) where on disembarkation, specimens of every animal and bird are sacrificed to God. Accordingly in order to ensure the survival of the species, more than one pair is required. Unclean animals are not similarly threatened because under ancient taboos they could not be sacrificed (Leviticus 11; Deuteronomy 14). P regarded the distinction between clean and unclean animals as unimportant because for him sacrifice and the laws regulating it only became operative following their disclosure to Moses at Sinai (Exodus 25ff.). Before that there was no legitimate Yahweh cult. This explains his simple reference to pairs in Genesis 6:19.

A further difference between P's theology and J is that the latter pictures the flood in purely naturalistic terms, forty days and nights of torrential rain. The cosmic dimension in the narrative is entirely due to P's theology, which also relies on a complicated but precise system of dating, the significance of which is now lost to us.

(vi)

How is the flood described?

The bulk of the flood narrative leading to the grounding of the vessel (Gen. 7:6–8:6) is from the Priestly Writer, though evidence of J language and thought appears throughout. It is, however, subservient to P theology derived from his creation account. By making Noah six hundred years old when the flood begins, the Priestly Writer ensures that all the long-lived patriarchs of his genealogy in Genesis 5 are dead. In contrast to J's forty days and forty nights, the P flood lasts one year and ten days in the Hebrew text, and exactly one year in the Greek.

Unlike the Epic of Gilgamesh where the gods themselves become frightened by their own actions, God is pictured as entirely in control of events. He shuts Noah, his family and the animals in the vessel, and proceeds through the flood waters to destroy all life on earth. Then he re-creates in the same manner as before. A wind which recalls the divine wind of Genesis 1:2 blows over the flood waters to dry them up, and the waters above and below the firmament are stopped. But while the Priestly Writer again preserves ancient concepts, no idea of a battle with the forces of chaos survives. The flood is sent at God's direction, and ceases at his command. So the vessel grounds on the mountains of Ararat, probably the highest range known to the Hebrews.

What is the significance of the J conclusion to the flood narrative?

Genesis 8:6–13 describes how Noah knew when it was safe to disembark. As in the Epic of Gilgamesh, birds are released to find out whether the flood has subsided. These were frequently used in ancient times as aids to navigation to see whether land was near. Clearly J assumes that Noah cannot see what is going on: so he lets the dove out of a hatch in the roof to find out. On the other hand the raven, which has no essential part in the story, is pictured as being watched by Noah flying up and down outside the vessel until it disappears, so indicating that it has found somewhere on land to settle. The bird belongs to the P vessel with its window (Gen. 6:16).

The record of Noah's disembarkation from the vessel is part of P, but one further J fragment remains in the account of Noah's sacrifice (Gen. 8:20–22), which as in the Epic of Gilgamesh, marks the climax of J's flood narrative. But there is no thought here of Noah attempting to placate God. The flood is already over. Noah's sacrifice is a free thank-offering which God unashamedly enjoys to the full, and secures that union between God and man which is the aim of all sacrifice. Through his enjoyment, God recognizes that man is an essential component of his own life whose destruction would cause him loss. While he knows that man's nature has not altered as a result of the flood—that not only has he the capacity to do evil, but the intention too—none the less he cannot renounce him. J thus affirms the important theological truth of both Judaism and Christianity that God needs man as much as man needs God. It is not just that man must co-operate with God in order that the garden can be tended, God's kingdom come: it is also that there is a positive enjoyment for both God and man in their relationship. They can literally delight in each other's company. So J recognizes that God must accept the consequences of that mystery which occurred in creation whereby he was able to pronounce it good, yet the snake was able to ensure man's rebellion.

Proof that God will not renounce man is given in the unchanging pattern of the seasons and days. Behind this declaration lies the primitive fear of the dying of the earth in summer and of the day at sunset. With the autumn rain and the dawn respectively, dark and destructive forces are defeated with new life and light. But for J, behind this continuous cycle of life the Hebrews were to see the God who had elected them in constant control of events and ever exercising his grace towards them. This J theology exactly coincided with the Priestly Writer's, which explains why P retains what is in his view an anachronistic reference to sacrifice. He has allowed himself to pass from primaeval times to his own when through the proper worship of the cult alone, the God-man relationship was to be sustained for all time. J's insight is thus confirmed by P, though both theologians recognize that it is due to no merit on man's part who remains intent on evil, but on God's grace alone.

(viii)

What is the significance of the P conclusion to the flood narrative?

Genesis 8:13a records that it was on New Year's Day that the waters began to dry up. This may reflect a cultic background, for many scholars have argued for a pre-exilic New Year Festival in ancient Israel inherited from Canaan on which the triumph of God over the forces of chaos was celebrated. But there still remains considerable doubt concerning such a festival, the existence of which is nowhere mentioned in any pre-exilic historical or liturgical text. Though certain Psalms are often interpreted in the light of such a festival, one cannot use such an interpretation to prove its existence. But as in Genesis 1:1–2:4a, the Priestly Writer may be consciously drawing on a Babylonian background—the New Year festival celebrating Marduk's struggle against chaos—which he then subjects to his own monotheistic theology.

Noah, his family and the animals disembark from the vessel and God renews his commission to them to breed and multiply (cp. Gen. 1:20–28). The Priestly Writer thus continues his theme of re-creation. The flood has marked a radical break with all that has gone before, and for P indicates the discontinuity between the pre- and post-exilic periods. As we shall see, in one sense things can never be the same again (Gen. 9:1–7). Sin always leaves its consequences behind: the world is not the same place as it was before. But there is continuity too. Noah and his family have been saved, and a new order can be established related to the old Israel though distinct from it (Ezekiel 37). This is where P's theology, which recognizes both continuity and discontinuity, differs markedly from the Deuteronomists. For the latter any future for Israel could only be contemplated on the terms given to the pre-exilic community, namely that their future existence depended solely on obedience to God's law. The Deuteronomists' hope centres on a possible replaying of the past—giving Israel another chance. But the Priestly Writer sees the unsatisfactory nature of such a second-chance theology, for it offered nothing in the face of further disobedience, but continued to threaten the future existence of Israel's relationship with her God. For P election was not something which could be terminated, for long before the Christian era, P recognized the theological truth that God could not change his nature. As St John was to proclaim, God is love and can be no other (1 John 4:8). For P, God having elected Israel, though he could and would punish her, could not abandon her. Her election stands, and the covenant with Noah (Gen. 9:8–17) indicates that it will do so for all time—unless Israel wilfully refuses to recognize it. This is always P's fear. So in the face of the alternative Deuteronomic theology, P adopts and confirms the insights of J's understanding of Israel's relationship with her God—using the same literary form of specifying the sin, its punishment, its consequences, and the further exercise of God's grace, thereby reinforcing the cyclic appearance of Genesis 1–11. So the sin of the generation of the flood leads to punishment and a changed environment: but God's grace is not withdrawn—indeed its reaffirmation enables men to live in the worsened situation which their sin has brought upon them.

Genesis 9:1–7 describes the world as no longer the idyllic place it was created to be: instead the animals live in fear of man who can legitimately kill them for food. For P, the end of vegetarianism is then a necessary evil though even here man is not given an entirely free hand: the blood of the animal must first be drained from it. As we have seen (p. 32), the Hebrews recognized that death occurred through loss of breath or blood, and since God was responsible for creation, both must belong to him. Consequently whenever meat was eaten, the animal was taken to the local sanctuary for slaughter, its blood being poured out on the altar and so returned to God. Later, following the centralization of all worship at Jerusalem and the consequent destruction of local sanctuaries (2 Kings 23) this duty became impracticable, and the killing of animals for food was secularized. This could still be undertaken locally but the blood had first to be poured out on the earth (Deuteronomy 12:20f.). While the Holiness

Code (Leviticus 17–26), written just before the exile and incorporated into P, may have attempted to reverse this secularization (Leviticus 17:1–14) in fact the totally changed conditions of post-exilic Israel prevented this. To this day orthodox Jews only eat meat from which the blood has been drained.

This discussion on blood leads P on to reiterate the ancient law of murder in which he clearly has J's account in Genesis 4 in mind. As we saw there (p. 32), when a man was killed his murderer was thought to gain possession of his blood which properly belonged to God, the seeker of blood (Gen. 9:5), and which cried to him for release from its captor (Gen. 4:9f.; Job 16:18). This could only be achieved through the execution of the murderer (Exodus 21:12), which applied even if the killing was done by an animal. So the law of the goring ox (Exodus 21:28) lays down that the ox is to be executed by stoning to death—the normal method of judicial execution in ancient Israel. As P reiterates, man was made in the image of God (Gen. 1:26–27), for relationship with him, and is therefore God's alone. But when there was a duty to execute, the blood of the victim would not pass into the hands of the executioners (Leviticus 20:9ff.; Joshua 2:19; 2 Samuel 1:16; 1 Kings 2:37). This was also the case in war, in which the blood of the slaughtered foe was seen as being devoted to God whose war it was.

Genesis 9:7 emphasizes again the duty of man to procreate, the fulfilment of which was seen as a sign of God's blessing (Job 42:16). But the vision of the animal world living at peace was not lost, the return to the idyllic state of Eden becoming the subject of the prophetic hope of the messianic age (Isaiah 11:6–9), for Christians to be realized at the end of time (Romans 8:18–25).

P concludes the flood narrative with the inauguration of the covenant with Noah (Gen. 9:8–17) already heralded at Genesis 6:18. This is the climax of his account through which he reiterates by another creative act the exilic community's unequivocable election by God.

The term 'covenant' (berith) defines a binding relationship between two parties (Gen. 31:44) in which obligations may be placed on one or both of them. In J, God was held to have bound himself by a covenant with Abraham (Gen. 15) through which he would ensure that Abraham became the father of a great nation (Gen. 12:1–3). This covenant was seen as fulfilled in the covenant with David and his heirs (2 Samuel 7) and the establishment of the Davidic-Solomonic empire which J's literary work celebrates. Neither on Abraham nor

David were obligations laid: God had elected them by an act of sheer grace, grace which other people would enjoy, for through Abraham (and now the Davidic empire) all peoples would find themselves blessed (pp. 60f.).

But Deuteronomic theology challenged the notion of an unconditional covenant. Instead at Sinai God was understood to have laid obligations on Israel, whose failure to fulfil them had resulted in the exile. But P by taking the idea of the covenant back before Abraham into the primaeval era sought to reiterate that God had voluntarily bound himself not just to Israel, but to mankind (*adam*) as a whole, irrespective of mankind's response to him. Indeed the covenant with Noah is made with the whole created order: it is the one God's pledge to his creation, his declaration of assent to it for all time. And to confirm this, he performs a further act of creation not included in his work on the six days in Genesis 1: he makes the rainbow. As with the mark on Cain's forehead in Genesis 4, this sign indicates that men can ever depend on him for their protection. While even within the Old Testament there are traces of the mythological idea of the rainbow as a weapon of God (Lamentations 2:4, 3:12), P shows nothing of this. Instead he uses the rainbow as he used the sabbath (Gen. 1:1–2:4a) and was to use circumcision (Gen. 17), as a sign of irrevocable commitment to Israel and through her to all peoples.

So the prophet of the exile we call Second Isaiah (Isaiah 40–55) uses the three covenants of grace, Noah (Isaiah 54:9–10), Abraham (Isaiah 51:2–3) and David (Isaiah 55:3) to indicate the everlasting and unconditional nature of God's election of Israel. Even now her salvation signified by her return to her own land was at hand, a salvation which would have universal significance as through her deliverance all nations came to acknowledge her God (Isaiah 49:6, 55:5) and his law (Isaiah 42:4). For Christianity this vision was to be realized by the nations coming through the waters of baptism (Matthew 28:19) to life in the new covenant inaugurated by Jesus (1 Peter 3:20–21).

Chapter 8

The Sons of Noah (Gen. 9:18–10:32)

(i)

Who were the sons of Noah?

Both in his genealogy (Gen. 5:32) and in his flood narrative (Gen. 6:10, 7:13) P has named the three sons of Noah as Shem, Ham and Japheth, presumably in the order of their births, a tradition which he inherited from J (Gen. 9:18). But in the J story of the drunkenness of Noah, Ham is described as the youngest son (Gen. 9:24) and in the cursing and blessing formula (Gen. 9:25) he is replaced by Canaan. Genesis 9:22 which names Ham as the father of Canaan is clearly an attempt to get round these difficulties which only partially succeeds. Perhaps there was an older tradition that Canaan was the son of Noah, which later came to be thought inappropriate for such a righteous ancestor.

While the perspective of the P genealogy in Genesis 10 is universalistic, the descent of all the peoples of the world being traced back to the three sons of Noah, the cursing and blessing formula has a much more limited outlook, concentrating on the situation in Palestine at the time J wrote. The Canaanites, whose land the Hebrews had entered, are cursed to be the most servile of all peoples, and the Hebrews themselves blessed through their ancestor Shem, the father of the Semites. The identity of the people represented by Japheth remains another problem. His blessing, using a pun on his name, the Hebrew word for 'enlarge' being *japht,* implies that another people combined with the Israelites in taking over Canaan and subjecting the indigenous population to their rule.

The most obvious candidate is the Philistines, those sea people from Caphtor (Amos 9:7; Jeremiah 47:4; cp. Gen. 10:14), definitely identified with Crete, who failing to find a foothold in Egypt, settled on the coastal plain of Palestine and came into conflict with the Hebrews when they sought to move into the hill country (Judges 14ff.; 1 Samuel 4). It was only after the defeat of Saul at Mount Gilboa (1 Samuel 31) that David managed to check their advance (2 Samuel 8:1). But Philistia remained unconquered by Israel throughout the Davidic-Solomonic period when J wrote, although subdued by Egypt whose Pharaoh gave Canaanite Gezer to Solomon as a wedding dowry (1 Kings 9:16). It is possible that for J the failure to occupy all Canaan proved an embarrassment, as it seems clear that in Hebrew tradition the intended western boundary of the promised land was to be the Mediterranean sea (Joshua 15:12), though it was recognized that this ideal had never been realized (Joshua 13). J may then be anxious to explain why Philistia continued to co-exist beside Israel. This was not due to failure on God's part to give Israel her promised territory: it had never been intended that she should have the land of Japheth, as the patriarch Noah had indicated by his blessing. The difficulty about this explanation is the doubt that an avowedly nationalistic writer like J could have allowed the patriarchal hero to have blessed the uncircumcised Philistines with the invocation that their boundaries be enlarged so that they might dwell in the tents of Israel (Shem).

There is, however, a further possibility, that under Solomon's policy of making alliances with neighbouring powers, Philistia and Israel had entered into a treaty which recognized the former's independence. Perhaps there is a hint of this in 1 Kings 2:39–40 where a prominent Hebrew citizen, Shimei of Jerusalem, is able to recover two runaway slaves from Achish, the ruler of the Philistine city of Gath. Indeed it has been argued that under Solomon, Philistia was a vassal of Israel. All this remains very uncertain, and illustrates again how the Hebrew scriptures were written at a particular time for a particular people in a particular situation. We cannot always recover what that was, though it is clear that J's cursing and blessing narrative reflected a political situation familiar enough for those for whom he wrote. Further, whoever Japheth was, the author's main concern is to assert the Hebrews' triumph over the indigenous Canaanite population, a triumph which the capture of the Jebusite city of Jerusalem and its designation as the capital of the Davidic state of Israel proclaimed (2 Samuel 5:6ff.).

(ii)

Why is Canaan cursed?

The account of the drunkenness of Noah (Gen. 9:20–21) explains the pun on his name in Genesis 5:29 (p. 38). But no ethical judgement is being made on Noah's state. While there were for long certain groups in Israel hostile to the settled agricultural life in Canaan and preferring the nomadic tent-dwelling existence of the desert period, the Rechabites (Jeremiah 35) and Nazirites (Amos 2:11f.), neither of whom drank wine, there is no such thought in the J narrative which all along has pictured man as settled and engaged in agricultural work. Rather the J account simply records the scientific fact that Noah discovered what were the properties of wine and its consequent dangers. But wine itself remained a blessing for which Noah himself is responsible (cp. Psalm 104:15).

It is Ham the father of Canaan—and so by implication Canaan—who commits an offence. While Genesis 9:22 describes Ham as having seen his naked father—nakedness always being considered improper (2 Samuel 6:20)—in Genesis 9:24 Noah recognizes that Ham has actually done something to him. Although the author is unwilling to spell out the appalling details of what this act was, it must have been more than an immodest looking at his father's private parts. Rather what it seems is being passed over in hurried silence is Noah's actual seduction while unconscious. If this is so then J is deliberately asserting that there should be no surprise over the abhorrent sexual practices with which the Canaanites were habitually associated and which the Hebrews were to avoid (Leviticus 18:7ff. (see vv. 24ff.); 20:10ff. (see vv. 22ff.)), for their founder himself was guilty of the most unspeakable perversion perpetrated on the very person whom he should have respected above all men.

In Genesis 9:28 we return to the P genealogy broken off at Genesis 5:32 and continued in Genesis 10.

(iii)

What is the purpose of Noah's genealogy?

Genesis 10 is predominantly the work of P, though as in the flood narrative he augments and supplements his genealogy from J material (Gen. 10:8–19,21,24–30). His purpose is to indicate how Noah fulfilled the divine command to be fruitful and multiply (Gen. 9:1). The diverse multitude of the nations all descended from one man is a further sign of God's blessing on the righteous patriarch. Having noted again the names of Noah's sons, Shem, Ham and Japheth, P traces their descendants in reverse order, so reaching a climax with the line of Shem from whom the Israelites traced their origin.

The nations are classified neither by race nor language, but location. Roughly speaking the sons of Japheth are the peoples of the north and west, the sons of Ham the peoples of the south, and the sons of Shem the peoples of the east, Palestine being at the centre of the author's compass. But the point which P is making is neither geographical nor historical, but theological. By deliberately placing no emphasis on Israel, P asserts that she is simply one among many nations (cp. Amos 9:7). There is then no inherent reason why she should be given world pre-eminence. Whatever status she acquires is not due to her natural ability and resources: rather it rests solely on God's election of her (Deuteronomy 7:7–8). It was this unmerited election which formed the core of P's theology and was adopted by other exilic and post-exilic theologians to prophesy that all nations would come and acknowledge Israel, and through her the one God from whom they all took their origin (Isaiah 2:2–4//Micah 4:1–4 (probably post-exilic); Isaiah 49:6, 55:5, 61:5–7; Zechariah 8:20–23).

(iv)

What is the significance of J's historical notes?

Various attempts have been made to identify Nimrod (Gen. 10:8–9), the most probable being Tukulti-Ninurta I, the first conqueror of Assyria in the thirteenth century. In Micah 5:6 Assyria is described as the land of Nimrod. He is pictured in Genesis 10 as the first absolute ruler, of whom, by P's time, Israel had known many. Perhaps it is significant that totalitarian rule is associated with Assyria. In Israel the king held his throne as a constitutional not an absolute monarch and was subject to the law (2 Samuel 12; Deuteronomy 17:18–20) which he was to uphold (Psalm 72). So Solomon built a special porch from which he could dispense justice (1 Kings 7:7).

In a brief historical allusion, Peleg's name is again explained as a pun, for in his time the world was divided (*palag*). This may refer forward to J's account of the division of the nations following the building of the tower of Babel (Gen. 11:1–9). But it has also been suggested from Isaiah 32:2 where *peleg* refers to water channels, that J may see Peleg as the originator of irrigation systems which naturally divide up the land.

J is also responsible for introducing Eber (Gen. 10:21,24–25), the ancestor after whom the Hebrews are named. It is probable that originally 'Hebrew' was not an ethnic term but referred to a particular

54

social or political group. It is related to the term Habiru or Apiru widely known throughout the ancient Near East and found in the fifteenth and fourteenth century Amarna letters where the Habiru threaten the Canaanite city states loyal to Egypt. While scholars have frequently identified these Habiru with brigands and outlaws, it is perhaps best to understand them as those who withdraw from an existing political system. So in 1 Samuel 14:21 we find rebel Israelites who had joined the Philistines designated as Hebrews. Hebrew would then be an apt description for those who had fled from political domination in Egypt. While no comment is made about the name Eber in Genesis 10, its presence in the genealogy would hardly have passed unnoticed.

Chapter 9

The Conclusion of the Primaeval Narrative (Gen. 11:1–12:3)

(i)

What is the purpose of the tower of Babel story?

Once more J reiterates his theme of the violation of the necessary separation of the heavenly and earthly realms. While man's rebellion against his human limitations is again used to explain another unpleasant fact of life, J's overall purpose is to repeat his theological pattern of sin, its punishment, its consequences—followed by yet another act of divine grace, the call of Abraham.

J's story is beautifully constructed, illustrating again what a superb artist he is. For the language used to describe man's assault on heaven (Gen. 11:1–4) is precisely repeated in the account of God's reversal of his plans (Gen. 11:5–9). Once more J sets his material in the mysterious east, this time in ancient Babylon pictured as man's first city and about which he had heard strange tales. Instead of the normal building materials of stone and mortar, Babylonian builders used brick and bitumen. Most prominent of these brick buildings were the ziggurats, large pyramid structures surmounted by a temple where it was thought a god dwelt and where men, by climbing the stepped sides, could be assured of meeting with the divine. Such was the background to J's narrative of man's last desperate attempt to gain access to the heavenly realm which instead resulted in the total breakdown of his intended unity.

Ironically J notes that it was fear that God intended to scatter men throughout the world that led them to try and thwart him by building a city with a tower stretching into heaven, and so usurping God's authority over them by becoming themselves like the *elohim* who dwelt there (Gen. 3:22). As J had already made God anticipate (Gen. 8:2), man's nature had in no way changed as a result of the flood. But would God's?

As in the Eden narrative (Gen. 3:8) of which Genesis 11:1–9 is virtually a theological re-play, God is not thought of as resident in the earthly realm, but visits it from time to time to see how man is carrying out his divine commission to order it. On such an inspection, God finds that once more men are challenging his authority by attempting to become 'like one of us'. So he summons the divine court to report this latest rebellion and to organize retaliatory action (cp. Gen. 3:22) against this potential threat to bridge earth and heaven. This action takes the form of confusing men's common language so making it impossible for them to plot together to become like the *elohim*. Indeed this sudden inability to communicate meant that they could not even finish off building their city (Gen. 11:8). J's narrative thus explains why men, although descended from a common ancestor, do not have a common language, something which the P genealogy had taken for granted (Gen. 10:5,20,31). But for J, like the other unpleasant facts of life—the pain of childbirth and the slog of farming (Gen. 3:16–19)— man's diverse languages are understood as the direct result of his arrogant attempt to know as God knows. As a result only God can understand each and every man. While man was made 'like one of us', and so unlike the animal world, given the ability to communicate with the divine realm, his attempt to grasp at divinity by becoming 'like one of us' results in divine judgement which further reduces his earthly power. But again there is no thought of a doctrine of original sin: man still remains constituted as he was intended to be, made in the image of God—that is, despite his confinement within the earthly realm, made to know and be known by him.

What is the purpose of Shem's genealogy?

P closely models the genealogy of Shem (Gen. 11:10–26) on his earlier genealogy of Adam (Gen. 5). The latter had recorded ten generations from creation to the flood, ending with Noah. Genesis 11:10–26 records a further ten generations from the flood to Abraham.

Genesis 5			Genesis 11:10–26		
Genealogy of Adam			*Genealogy of Shem*		
Adam			Shem		
Seth			Arpachshad		
Enosh			Shelah		
Kenan			Eber		
Mahalalel			Peleg		
Jared			Reu		
Enoch			Serug		
Methuselah			Nahor		
Lamech			Terah		
Noah		Abraham	Nahor		Haran
Shem	Ham	Japheth			

But as the Greek Septuagint recognized, the symmetry was not exact. For while Genesis 5 ends with the note that Noah, the tenth patriarch, fathered three sons, Genesis 11 has Abraham, the tenth patriarch, as one of the three sons of Terah, the ninth patriarch. Consequently the Septuagint introduces a further patriarch into the list in order to make the parallel with Genesis 5 exact—ten patriarchs of whom the tenth fathers three sons.

P uses the J information included in Genesis 10:21,24–25 which covers the first five patriarchs down to Peleg, at which point J breaks off to deal with Peleg's brother Joktan, and his descendants. P has then to complete for himself Shem's genealogy down to Abraham, though the absence of any J record of this after Peleg does not necessarily mean that J had not preserved the full list. As in Genesis 5 there is a marked difference in the numbers between the Hebrew, Greek and Samaritan versions, though the significance of this is no longer clear.

But P makes one deliberate distinction in his presentation of the two genealogies. While in Genesis 5 all the patriarchs before Noah die before the flood, and therefore escape God's judgement, in Genesis 11 all the patriarchs including Noah are alive at Abraham's birth and so witness the fulfilment of God's promises to Noah to be reaffirmed by P in the covenant of circumcision with Abraham (Gen. 17).

Many of the names in the genealogy have a North-West Mesopotamian background, and it is with this region inhabited by the early Aramaean peoples that the patriarchs are linked in Hebrew tradition (Deuteronomy 26:5). It was from Haran that Abraham was to set out on his journey to Canaan (Gen. 12:4), and so begin the fulfilment of God's reversal of the disastrous primaeval history of Genesis 1–11.

(iii)

What is the purpose of Terah's genealogy?

Genesis 11:27–32 is again an amalgam of J (vv. 28–30) and P (vv. 27, 31–32). Its purpose is to provide the essential background to the call of Abraham. First Abraham's immediate family is described in detail including the fact that his wife Sarah was barren. By giving away this fact before the call narrative, J makes God's blessing of Abraham as the father of a great nation (Gen. 12:2) seem distinctly inappropriate. How could this be? We know that it can only happen through direct divine intervention.

And second, although Abraham's journey to Canaan started from Haran (Gen. 12:4), his origins are clearly stated as lying in southern Mesopotamia at Ur of the Chaldees. This appellation is an anachronism in the narrative, for the Chaldeans only appear in southern Mesopotamia long after the supposed time of Abraham. But the introduction of Ur of the Chaldees is due entirely to P, even in J's verse 28, for the J tradition only knew of Abraham's home as in Haran (Gen. 12:4). P's purpose was to remind the exilic generation that as Abraham, the father of the nation, had come from the land of the Chaldeans, so the exilic generation to whom P wrote would also come from Chaldean territory to populate again the promised land. So Abraham acts for P as a sign of the continuity of the the covenant of grace which was God's will for his people. Even in the uncertainty of the exilic situation, God's promise to the patriarch remains valid (cp. Isaiah 51:2–3).

What is the importance of the call of Abraham?

J's narrative has been a repetitive story of constant refusal by man to accept his earthly limitations. Each successive incident has led to ever-widening repercussions until the situation is reached when the unity of mankind is shattered and men find themselves isolated from each other in a hostile world. Yet even now man's rebellion is answered by divine grace: God calls Abraham and the process of the reunification of mankind begins.

The call of Abraham (Gen. 12:1–3) is then both the climax of the tower of Babel story and of Genesis 1–11 as a whole, and it acts as the introduction to the story of man's salvation which J saw fulfilled in the Solomonic empire, and P anticipated in a restored Israel. Like Adam and Eve's clothes (Gen. 3:21) and Cain's mark (Gen. 4:15), the call of Abraham is God's reply to man's sin. As the scope of man's sin steadily increases throughout Genesis 1–11, so does the exercise of God's grace (Romans 5:20). This is the nature of the God who created man, and who cannot let him go, a nature which the Hebrew author whom we call J recognized three thousand years ago.

So by taking one man from the scattered nations God sets in motion the reversal of Genesis 1–11, the reunification of mankind within the garden of delight. But paradoxically this process though assured by God's unconditional promise to Abraham is not automatic: God depends on man's response. Abraham must abandon the security of Haran and set out for an unknown destination (Hebrews 11:8). Man's salvation can only be won by man committing himself in faith to the God who promises it, though of necessity this means letting go of the known and embracing the unknown. From the time of Eden, God has depended on man's co-operation—man limited to what he can know in the earthly realm. On his own God can achieve nothing, for he has given man dominion in that earthly realm. But man can only win his salvation by co-operating with the God who wills it for him and will not let him go until it is secured.

As the language of Genesis 12:1–3 indicates, J has modelled his blessing of Abraham on royal liturgical usage associated with the Davidic covenant (2 Samuel 7). This assured the king of numerous offspring, a great name and dominion over the nations (Psalms 2, 45, 72, 89). J has applied this royal ideology to the patriarch Abraham, and then seen the promise fulfilled in the Solomonic state whose order and magnificence seemed to echo Eden itself. Significantly when the Davidic kings failed to live up to such a vision, it became the subject of messianic hope (Isaiah 11).

For J the Solomonic splendour acted as an example of divine blessing to all nations who could only ask that God might bless them in the same way. This is the meaning of the final words of verse 3, that by Abraham all the families of the earth will bless themselves. But for P and the exilic theologians it was through Abraham that the other nations would acquire their blessing (Isaiah 49:6, 55:5, 61:5–7; Zechariah 8:20–23) by the exilic generation remaining faithful and appropriating for itself the covenant which God had made with Abraham. Only in this way could the nations inherit the blessing of Abraham (Ecclesiasticus 44:21; Acts 3:25; Galatians 3:8). While J celebrated the realization of God's salvation plans in the fulfilment of the promise to Abraham in the Solomonic empire, the outcome for P remained hesitant. The promise stood, but it was for the exilic generation to fulfil.

Chapter 10

Conclusions

(i)

What is the message of Genesis 1–11?

The repetitive nature of Genesis 1–11 almost makes a summary of its contents unnecessary. The authors' aim has been to present to their readers in the very different situations in which they found themselves, the nature of God, the nature of man and the nature of the relationship between them—none of which alters, no matter how different one's personal circumstances are. This marks the timelessness of Genesis 1–11, which remains an accurate analysis of the conditions under which faith has to be lived out two thousand five hundred years after its composition.

As part of creation, man remains earth-bound and can know nothing outside the earthly realm. Within it he has the duty to discover its order and exercise control over it. Indeed, without his active participation God remains impotent, for he has given man dominion over creation. Man can choose to co-operate in establishing that order which God declared good, or he can reject it. But to go against the divine order can only result in the marring of creation itself, the experiencing of more unpleasant facts of life. Nor in this respect are Christians in any different position from the people of the Old Testament. As the body of Christ, it is for them to bring about the inauguration of that kingdom for which at their Lord's command they daily pray. So for the nuclear age, Genesis 1–11 remains required reading.

The authors of Genesis 1–11 make no attempt to gloss over man's condition. He is intent on evil, an intention which finds expression in his refusal to accept his creaturely state. He resents the limits under which God had decreed that he should exercise his faith and seeks to step outside them—to be *elohim*. But faith can only be expressed agnostically: man cannot know as God knows. There is no certainty that the God to whom man commits himself in faith has not in fact tricked him—that he is no more than dust; that the vision of the idyllic garden is nothing but a hoax. The choice before man remains either to eat and drink, for tomorrow we die (Isaiah 22:13) or to strive for that world in which even the farthest places will be brought under God's

62

torah and so acknowledge his will (Isaiah 42:4), to seek the restoration of that garden where wild and domestic animals lie down together in peace and children play in safety by snakes' nests (Isaiah 11:6–9). Nothing which science can discover will remove this necessity of choice between co-operation with or rejection of God, or alter the conditions under which that choice must be made. For as the authors of Genesis 1–11 assert, it must always be exercised against the background of those two aspects of divinity which man can never have and with which science is powerless to provide him—the knowledge of good and evil, and immortality. But by forbidding man such fruit and telling him that he had done so, God made it possible for man to have a relationship with him. Had he been allowed to eat such fruit unchecked, he would have had no choice but to have been a heavenly robot: had he never heard of such fruit, he would have shared the status of earthly animals. Instead he experiences, as he does with his fellow men, the risk of relationship, the abandonment to the other in faith, a faith which can never become proof while man remains within the earthly realm.

Yet it is always man's peculiar sin to avoid his true condition, the necessary expression of agnostic faith. Either he says with the fool of the Psalm, there is no God (Psalm 14:1, 53:1), or like Job's friends he denies the conditions under which faith must be exercised by providing all the answers. But man must practise his faith in the earthly realm in which God has expressly denied him the answers both to the origin of evil and what happens after death. The wise sceptic is right: today we eat and tomorrow we die. But the question which faces *adam* is under what circumstances do we eat—which leads, as I stated in the Preface, to the fundamental question raised by Genesis 1–11: Have you the courage to believe in your own salvation?

It will indeed need courage, for man must exercise his belief against the background of unremitting suffering, much of it not his responsibility, and in the end the blankness and meaninglessness of death. But in the face of this stark reality, the authors of Genesis 1–11 assert that both in good times (J) and in bad (P) God wills to know man and no matter what atrocities man commits will not desert him. As the Hebrew wise knew, to fail to co-operate with the divine order must inevitably lead to suffering, but as P reaffirmed to the exilic generation, no man can by his own efforts put himself beyond the love of God, for every man is made in his image. For Christians the cross confirms God's love. The arms of the crucified one who did not grasp at being 'like one of us' but who alone realized to the full his being made 'like one of us', stretch out to embrace *adam*. In those arms at-one-ment is achieved for God and man.

(ii)

Does anything else need to be said?

But one thing remains to be said which is not said in Genesis 1–11, and that is how the garden is to be re-entered, the kingdom come. Throughout Genesis 1–11 man's rebellion results in loss of what was previously his to enjoy. So Adam and Eve are expelled from the garden (Gen. 3:23–24), Cain is driven into exile (Gen. 4:14), and the people of Babel are scattered all over the earth (Gen. 11:8). But paradoxically the reversal of this process of the disintegration of mankind can also only be realized by loss, this time not as a punishment for sin, but by the voluntary abandonment ˙ of one's security in faith, by self-annihilation. So in the first act of man's history of salvation, Abraham responds to God's call to leave Haran and abandons himself in faith, not knowing where he was to go (Gen. 12:1–3, Hebrews 11:8). Such voluntary abandonment is to be the pattern for all men of faith. So in God's own time Abraham is again brought to the test by the command to lift the sacrificial knife over his son Isaac, the child of promise (Gen. 22). By such faithful abandonment of all that he held most dear, Abraham showed that at no time does God's promise of salvation become automatic, for as the exilic generation were to realize, faith has continually to be lived out, continually reiterated through suffering and even death (Isaiah 53). While the future always depends on God's grace, that grace can only find expression through men of faith being prepared to act in faith when they no longer have any cause to do so.

So in that final act of the history of man's salvation, Jesus must die as we all will die alone and in ignorance, yet expressing his agnostic faith, for this is the only faith that man can have: My God, my God, why hast thou forsaken me? (Mark 15:34). He too could not know as God knows; he too must face the blankness of death. But he dies in faith, abandoning his life on the cross into his Father's hands: 'It is finished' (John 19:30). And it is this same cross which he bids his followers take up (Mark 8:34). To seek the coming of the kingdom in

64

any other way than the way of the cross is to mistake the very nature of the God whose grace will not let man go, whose arms are ever stretched to embrace all men.

Yet there are too many Christians who seek a short cut to resurrection, who find it easier to think of heaven hereafter than the cost of discipleship now. They prefer the empty cross to the cross with the tortured figure of the rabbi from Nazareth limp upon it. But the message of Old and New Testaments is that the garden cannot be re-entered, the kingdom come, save by faithful embracing of that cross of self-annihilation which makes resurrection possible. For there to be resurrection, there must be death first.

So like the timeless primaeval stories of Genesis 1–11, the cross too is more than an historical event, a date in time. The hope of *adam* lies not in any process of historical progress, in what he himself can achieve, but solely in the cross which once embraced allows God to achieve in him the miracle of resurrection which transformed and transforms history. Like the sign of the sabbath (Gen. 1:1–2:4a), the cross assures *adam* of his election, but only by appropriating it for himself can that election be realized. For the Christian to have the courage to believe in his own salvation inevitably means to take up the cross of self-annihilation, the cross of the second Adam, to share in the hopelessness of his death in order to partake of the fullness of his resurrection. And when *adam* has the courage to do that, he will find himself again in the garden of delight naked but unashamed. The kingdom will have come.

A Note on Further Reading

For a more detailed discussion of the issues raised by Genesis 1–11 commentaries should be consulted. Of these E. A. Speiser, *Genesis* (Anchor Bible), Doubleday and Co. 1966; G. von Rad, *Genesis* (Old Testament Library), SCM Press, 3rd edition 1972; Robert Davidson, *Genesis 1–11* (Cambridge Bible Commentary), Cambridge University Press 1973; Bruce Vawter, *On Genesis: A New Reading*, Geoffrey Chapman 1977 may be recommended.

On some of the theological issues found in Genesis 1–11, Brevard S. Childs, *Myth and Reality in the Old Testament*, SCM Press 1960; Claus Westermann, *Creation*, SPCK 1974; John Rogerson, *The Supernatural in the Old Testament*, Lutterworth Press 1976; Patrick D. Miller Jr, *Genesis 1–11* (*Journal for the Study of Old Testament* Supplement Series 8), University of Sheffield 1978 will prove helpful.

My own *God B.C.*, Oxford University Press 1977 fills out the background material.

Comparative material will be found set out in J. B. Pritchard, *Ancient Near Eastern Texts Relating to the Old Testament*, Princeton University Press, 3rd edition 1969; and D. Winton Thomas (ed.), *Documents from Old Testament Times*, Nelson and Sons 1958.

For Thought and Discussion

(Prepared by BRF.)

A.

1. The author says that Genesis 1–11 'gives the plot (of the Bible) away'. Do you find this a helpful way of understanding these opening chapters?

2. In what ways does our understanding of 'creation' express what we believe about God?

3. How does Jesus help us to see what it means to be truly human?

4. We are created in God's 'image' and yet need to accept 'those limitations which constitute the true human life'. In the modern world what limits are to be observed? When do we usurp God's prerogative?

5. In Genesis 4:1–5 notice:
   (a) that Cain by murdering Abel had literally 'taken his life', a life said to belong to God;
   (b) that Cain having 'taken' his brother's life denied any responsibility for it;
   (c) that God punished Cain but also protected him.
   What do these insights teach us about our responsibility for other people, and our attitude to the punishment of wrong-doers?

6. How might we re-write the essential meaning of Genesis 1–11 in terms of our contemporary society?

7. What is the value of family-trees? Why did the editor of Genesis 1–11 feel it important to insert genealogies?

8. Pentecost has been described as 'the tower of Babel turned upside down'. Read Acts 2:1–11 and try to imagine you are explaining it to the authors of Genesis 1–11.

67

B.

1. In the light of Dr Phillips' book as a whole, what do these chapters of Genesis indicate of the abiding significance of the Old Testament?

2. The Old Testament material was produced at particular times, by particular people, in particular situations—which we cannot now recover. Do reasoned expositions such as here (e.g. Noah 'as example to the exilic age') give the Scriptures new force and relevance?

3. What modern parallels are there to the differences between Deuteronomy's 'threat theology' and P's gospel of grace?

4. Because mankind presumes to be as God ('one of us'), 'the whole created order suffers'. How does this work out in practice? 'For the nuclear age, Genesis 1–11 remains required reading.'

5. Why do we so seldom appreciate the Old Testament on its own terms? Has the author's exposition of its gospel (no Fall but much grace) opened new vistas?

6. Fundamental problems in church unity and mission stem from varying ideas of what constitutes 'faith'. The lessons of Genesis 1–11 could clarify and reassure. Do you understand, and agree with, chapter 10's description of faith?

7. Free to choose, and at the same time determined by circumstances: do we accept this tension of the human predicament? How does faith in Christ enable us to live with it?

8. 'God is not man's to control.' Is the Jewish-Christian revelation a religion, or the end of all religions? In what ways has the whole of life become our religion?